REMAKE

Also by Christine Brooke-Rose from Carcanet

Brooke-Rose Omnibus
(Out / Such / Between / Thru)
Amalgamemnon
Xorandor
Verbivore
Textermination

REMAKE

CHRISTINE BROOKE-ROSE

CARCANET

First published in Great Britain in 1996 by
Carcanet Press Limited
402–406 Corn Exchange Buildings
Manchester M4 3BY

A CIP catalogue record for this book
is available from the British Library.
ISBN 1 85754 222 3

The publisher acknowledges financial assistance
from the Arts Council of England.

Set in 10½ pt Bembo by Bryan Williamson, Frome
Printed and bound in England by SRP Ltd, Exeter

1. REMAKE

The black car limousines along the colonnade.

The Secretary of State descends the White House steps towards the car-door held open onto a beige leathered emptiness, larger and larger as the viewer enters. The Secretary of State descends the airplane steps to be welcomed by the Russian Foreign Minister and delegation before being engulfed by the first of a waiting fleet. From the windows the viewer sees the sudden Kremlin surge. The overvoice continues to prognose problems to be discussed in the way of nuclear dismantling internal opposition for support at the UN in the present conflict elsewhere.

The viewer, an old lady of seventy-two, has professed literature, for twenty years as teacher in a Paris University but for forty years as writer, retired to Provence. The old lady knows this is routine remake, the cameraman having got into another limousine rented and drawn up for the purpose along the colonnade, into the beige leathered emptiness looming at the lens, into a no doubt small Trabant driving towards Moscow and the Kremlin.

But then, everything in the old lady's life is remake now, as is the world viewed in cartoon-strip. Mention of anything at all, person, place, problem, package deal, needs an image, a map a landscape a city a street a house a head, the Chancellor of the Exchequer at a desk in Number 11, turning the page of a large ledger by the open bright red dispatch-case, brand new, so unlike the darkened old dispatch-case displayed on Budget Day, black on old newsreels, blotched mahogany and yellow on TV. A new library picture has to be made whenever a new Chancellor is appointed. Images of ministers walking past the railings of Downing Street and into bobbied Number 10, the door opened

1

by an invisible hand, party leaders in the hall of the Assemblée Nationale, ministers shaking hands in Brussels, Edinburgh, Geneva, Rio, Corfu, standing at summity buffets about global warmongering awkwardly holding plate and glass or coming out to face a cluster of toffee-apples with a toffee statement carefully licked to say little, ponderously hesitating towards the expected clayshit and getting into a drawn-up limousine to drive away, external shot. The overvoice on the French news mistranslates: A la fin de la journée ... un accord. The old lady laughs alone, will check on the BBC an hour later, for clearly the English delegate has used the current fuzz-phrase At The End Of The Day, and no agreement will be reached that evening.

The old lady thinks about the techniques of fiction, now regularly used in documentary. Getting inside the mind of a character, seeing things the character sees, thinking things the character thinks, seeing the character as well. But the author of fiction knows the inside of the character's mind because the character has come out of the author's mind.

Not out of the author's mind comes a knock at the door. Rachid, one of the cherry-pickers, with an offering of cherries in a plastic bag, also wants to come and weed this evening, when the sun has cooled. Voices chattering from the green trees, invisible human birds on ladders, the cherry-orchards and the green regimented vineyards stretching far towards the wooded hills. How kind of Rachid, although the old lady has the friendly farmer's permission to steal.

Difficult to get into Rachid's mind through fragmentary Moroccan French. Rachid looks eighteen but is twenty-eight and has five children in Morocco.

The little girl, aged two, is singing *Sur le Pont d'Avignon* to daddy in the dining-room. The dining-room is in Chiswick, at the back of a long deep flat, 15 Fairlawn Court, in a dark red building overlooking Acton Green. The dining-room has chairs covered in dirty yellow plush. No, says mummy some forty years later at seventy-two, St John's Wood, not Chiswick, Joanne at three was left with granny and grandad in Geneva, Chiswick was later, with both children, several times. The old lady has no memory at all of St John's Wood at two.

So le pont d'Avignon only half exists, stretching out broken into the flat slow yellow Rhône, so tumbling green in Geneva.

BUT learning the pater noster and the alpha beta gamma delta at daddy's knee in the dining-room, Chiswick. And the pater noster in a dark red dressing-gown on the small triangular balcony of the drawing-room at the front of the house overlooking Acton Green. Pater noster waves goodbye to mummy bundling the two little girls into a big black cab on a last return to Brussels, in the long badminton of sending for and sending away. Is that a remake? Or a self-confrontation?

Self-confront many selves or one? A confrontation of two entities, as in the folk tale, a hero (small but cunning and brave) and a villain (huge but stupid and cowardly), or a white knight and a black in a murderous clanging joust, or at most a giant green knight and at mostest a flaming golden dragon? But the entities are not of equal status and stature, the confronter is a speck in time compared to the army of confrontable selves.

Clearly grammar supports self-confrontation. John[1] confronts John[1]. The rule of reflexivization requires a coreferentially repeated Noun Phrase in the deep structure to become pronominalized. And the definition of a personal pro-noun?

A pro-noun is an anti-noun, an anti-name, an anti-person.

A substitution.

A simulation.

An identification.

A possession and a dispossession.

Une fuite en avant.

Grammar doesn't say how many Johns or how many selves (and what colour), or whether some past Johns are confronting one present John or one present John is confronting one or all or a selection of past Johns.

John is whole languages. John has as many selves as utterances, virtual or realized, as many selves as there are words in lexicons, each word an aetiology, a phoneyetic fragility, with semiantic seachanges, infinite contiguities and tall spokes of paradismatic possibilities. John is the excitement, the pursuit of knowledge, the donor with the magical auxiliary, an eagle, a flying horse, an invisibility ring.

3

Sometimes the old lady hates John, for at the surface John is both eager and easy to please, but differently positioned in each case, agent and patient, the pleasing John or the pleased John, the eagle John and the uneasy invisible John. John builds a house but cannot be built by a house, John can't be admired by sincerity, nor can John elapse.

Flying planes can be dangerous.

The old lady quantums back to pronominalization. Surely no metaphors are possible on pronouns except grammatical metaphors, using the pronoun as noun the way Donne did, or Cummings an adverb as adjective the way American blacks do and vice versa in a pretty how town. *How how can a town be,* hower than another town? Bruxelles est une ville loin, the little girl once said, or is reported later to have said, on a long train journey in a wooden-seated third-class carriage from Geneva or Wherever to Brussels.

Having zapped to adverbs and fluffed out short grey hair, the old lady confronts the little girl with sidetracks, substitutions and simulations about pronouns. Some people never use the other's name, but Monsieur, Madame or darling or pussycat even in anger. Some parents replace the child's chosen name with a diminutive or an early mispronunciation. Some ill-mannered persons make jokey transformations of any unfamiliar name, and French news presenters colonize all foreign names into French phonetics, yet would not be pleased if the English rhymed Mitterand with brand or Juppé with yuppy or pronounced Dumas as dumb ass or Delors as delorse. And indeed were furious at the tabloid headline Up Yours, Delors. People are frightened of names. Of otherness.

The world confronts the world in cartoon-strips, sidetracks, substitutions and simulations. The world is violent but the cameras are never there for the violence, only afterwards for the damage and interviews. Why come and film the misery here, says a Bosnian woman to the journalists, when the world won't help? Or else, exceptionally, the cameras are there but botch. Kennedy lying in the car, the pope being raced away, Monica Seles after being stabbed on the tennis-court, surgical bombing on a surgical image from way up. Dying on the news is not allowed, only at most corpses. Yet there is a daily dousing of dastardly deaths in telefiction, viewers want those but would outcry at real dyings.

On Saturday evenings the old lady watches a programme on the French cultural channel called *Histoire parallèle* showing the newsreels of the same week fifty years ago, German, English, French, later American, Russian, Japanese. This is the world news in pictures, Pathé Gazette screening. With two historians hind-citing omissions and lies, the old lady hind-siting irrelevance, knocked into long lost images. The Germans use film-directors, slicing the distant or maybe mocked-up battle-scenes with brilliant close-ups of enthusiastic soldiers sailors airmen in tanks submarines cockpits, while the English make dubious jokes about Wops and Eyties, Huns and Jerries and cheerily show the king and queen visiting bomb damage, the home guard training, the football matches and war-fashions and factory-girls. Life is normal. Well, the Germans show all that too, and generals meeting and Hitler-youths in happy holiday-homes, more and more so as battles get lost and soldiers look more exhausted, less enthusiastic, just as the British later show more battles being won, as well as generals meeting plumply battle-dressed Churchill in North Africa and such. The German-ruled French revel in sport, and speeches delivered in a mixture of priestly intoning and Comédie Française declamation, a style retained by Malraux well into the sixties. In all the newsreels the voice is cracked and hysterically hearty. In all presentations, the naturalization of war, to loud European military marches or Beethoven or Wagner, even in Japan. Things have got cleverer, not truer.

The young WAAF officer sits in a hut, later in a brick building, reading and evaluating German messages all day for priority lists to the intercepters and cryptographers. So many keys, daily to be broken, as fast as possible, sometimes within minutes of emission. Einsatzbereitschaftsbericht, Einsatzmeldung, Einsatzbefehl, from Keitel to Kesselring, from Kesselring to Rommel, from Von Rundstedt to subordinate divisions, from divisions to smaller units. The otherness of the other learnt young, the real war, seen from the enemy point of view at nineteen, twenty, twenty-one, twenty-two. Like watching different national newses today.

5

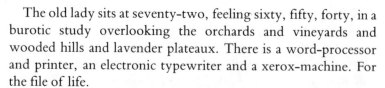

The old lady sits at seventy-two, feeling sixty, fifty, forty, in a burotic study overlooking the orchards and vineyards and wooded hills and lavender plateaux. There is a word-processor and printer, an electronic typewriter and a xerox-machine. For the file of life.

Why is the old lady trying to intercept all those interseptic messages? Old-age self-indulgence? No. The old lady's publisher has asked for an autobiography. But the resistance is huge. The absorbing present creates interference, as well as the old lady's lifelong prejudice against biographical criticism, called laundry-lists by Pound. Only the text matters, if the text survives at all. But the insistent request has needled the interception. In earlier days the image would have been more of a brain tossing in a launderette machine, a sort of brain-washing, often by mentors. Or a man-hoovering. But mentors come and go. There are no mentors now, except John, reaching Krafft ebbing through Freud by means of a magic Adler Fromm the Klein Jung. John is not easy to please, nor eagle neither, and seems to have elapsed after all.

On the roof is a vast dish, pivoting like an ear-eye to capture the news of the world, in English, American, German, French, Spanish, Italian, Polish, a monotonous variety of natiocentric views.

All the other programs are alike, intermediaocre, just as there are only four species of apples now, standardized taste, that is, none. The Wheel of Fortune, Glücksrad, the candidates doing all the work, cheaper than paying professionals, even with the prizes. Copfilms and violence. And long-amortized soap, old slices of life in fragmented scenes flung together, no dialogue more than two sentences, today's attention-span being about thirty seconds. Just like life. Some feminists, the old lady remembers, insisted on both flux and fragmentation as female specificity in art. Perhaps such feminists were reared on soap. The old lady also wonders why American soap is always about the very rich, European soap always about doctors and lawyers and journalists, and English soap always about the working-class. Perhaps only the workers watch, now there is no work, or only organised stupefying work requiring organized stupefied leisure.

But the dish is not for that, the dish is for watching the journalists provoking pseudo-events on the square of the high pother news, and the political behaviour of the participating public, so unaware of being manipulated for profit and crowd-controlled in the best thirties tradition: le bo-bo, le nu-nu, le?...BONUS! And the agonies of effort, the ecstasies of pain or joy on the faces of tennis-players, so different in essence from the bland banal interviews afterwards, like authors interviewed outside the book. For the first time in the old lady's life there is all the time in the world to watch the world, a world never watched before, not as professor, not as literary journalist, not as student, not, of course, as WAAF officer, a world totally strange though so familiar to all the rest of the world watching the world in blaring baring uncaring depairing detail. The dish keeps the old lady in touch with languages once known or half-known, and with English as now spoke: Having said that, hopefully at the end of the day the bottom line will be a level playing-field, on the line, but at the present time there's still a long way to go. Luckily there's also reading, for pleasure at last, not for an exam, a thesis, a review, a class, a seminar or a conference paper. The old lady is not yet going blind.

One day there will come the shrinkage into a smaller space, in England perhaps, on the Kentish coast maybe, a terraced cottage along the seafront in Hythe for example, facing the same grey Channel as once did the schoolroom and the dormitory of the semi-posh school on the cliffs above Hythe, the address nevertheless Folkestone to sound posher. One day or sometime soon, here after all maybe, there will have to come the helplessness, an old people's home, being lifted from the bed into the armchair with a catheter to sit head bent in an outward stare, an inward gaze. But for the moment there is still the world to be watched at last, in the unsparing detail of simulation.

The dish causes trouble with the neighbours on either side, Simone to the East, a psychoanalyst, and Suzie to the West, a painter, the two serpents according to the rest of the hamlet, well-matched, the two S's, gland in glove, S^1 and S^2, unco-referential.

The old lady doesn't meet Simone, petite and dark, until six months after settling there, seven years ago, at five o'clock on Christmas Eve, on Simone's doorstep. The old lady, a little younger then and newly retired, asks about psychoanalysis, maybe gushing about Lacan. But Simone is suddenly abrupt, Simone's son is about to arrive. That means no passing the threshold. Perhaps Simone is an anti-Lacanian. Of course, the old lady says, do both come round for a drink over Christmas.

The son isn't in fact arriving till the next day, and there's no coming round.

Six months later the old lady tries again. Sorry, plenty of friends already, no need for more. Plonk. But in a saccharine psychoanalytic tone.

Suzie has a large black dog, called Tor and kept in an enclosure, or muzzled when let out, but the dog nevertheless digs up all the gardens. Last year the old lady gets out of the car hot and exhausted after an absence visiting friends in Italy or maybe Janek, now friendly again at last, in Spain, and Suzie rushes out with a long story about Tor having jumped on the roof of the enclosure and got out. Suzie doesn't ask about the trip, or how the old lady is, the old lady is refused existence, but listens patiently, daring after a while to mention fatigue and the desire for a shower and a cup of tea. A shower and a cup of tea, that's real. Simone's house has a pipe sticking out and flooding the village lower down whenever the hose is used. The village mutters but doesn't complain. Live and let live. Oh, is that Israeli music, Simone asks breezily into the open window. No, says the old lady, Hungarian. Ah, says Simone, antisemitic, eh?

A curious form of humour perhaps. The old lady has given up all but polite greetings, wondering occasionally whether Simone is as rude with patients. But when the dish is put up, Simone calls with psycharine reproaches. Not in the style of the region. And no consultation either. The old lady admits the unprovençal effect, but replies dryly, if the neighbours had been more welcoming there would have been no need for spatial visitors. Ah bon, les voisins sont donc les méchants?

Simone and Suzie mount a kabal against the dish and this peculiar foreigner, not quite right in the head, but the rest of the hamlet, much more friendly, defends the old lady, the two enchanting old twins, retired astrologists, and old, sick Madame Bernard, visited often by the old lady, partly in real concern, but partly no doubt self-righteously to show neighbourliness as should be. What does that mean, say the twins, the whole region is up in arms? Has a house-to-house been done? And what about Simone's new garage opposite, with that pretentious false ruin of a wall sloping down sideways, blocking the view? Nobody was consulted on that. And what about the water, and what about the dog? Move with the times. And so on.

The local life opens no life. The flight from patriarchy is matriarched.

But then, things would presumably have been much the same if the old lady had retired in Kent. Used to big cities, where neighbours don't exist, only chosen friends. Big cities spoil people. Small villages reveal the self-enclosed: after the outpourings about dogs or grandchildren or illnesses or garden problems the self-enclosed abruptly stop and say alors, tout va bien? Au revoir.

The old lady has spanned almost the century, the end in anticipation, the beginning in hearsay, La Grande Guerre, le Kaiser, le roi Albert saying NON, les tranchées and horror, Verdun, Ypres, la Somme, nettle soup, la Guerre and Belgium the centre, though the grown-ups, the old lady now realizes, were not in Belgium at the time, grandpère, grand'mère and two sons in Geneva, the four daughters in America on girl jobs. And the same dramattitudes years later, after the second war, on a visit to the Geneva branch with Janek. What were things like during the Blitz? Well – Yes and every night the Allied planes could be heard rumbling over, on the way to bomb Italy! And there was no rice!

Schools teach a national version of history, but learning the history of Belgium in the thirties means learning the history of Europe, for Flanders belonged to many powers. Napoleon or Pépin le Bref, Charlemagne, the Duke of Burgundy, Maximilien d'Autriche, Charlequint, Philip II, le roi soleil, Guillaume d'Orange – le soleil an orange on some man's head like the apple on William Tell's. History is chiefly battles and the names of kings and alliance marriages lending legendary personality and glamour, the people being just armies moved on maps or rebels and riots put down. The little girl thinks how much easier to learn if kings and popes had the same numbers as the centuries reigned in, Louis the Ninth in the ninth, Gregory the Seventh in the seventh. True, some would have to share, Louis the Fifteenth and Sixteenth being the Eighteenth a and b.

For Belgium, apart from being a region called Belgica by the Romans, has only existed for a hundred years since 1830, *le belge sortant du tombeau*, heard so much more vividly as *tambour*. Childhood is strewn with mishearings and mistranslations, le lendemain is le lent demain, un fait divers is a winter fact, un pantouflard is a slippery fellow, the flick of a coin is le flic du coin, une arrière-pensée an afterthought, a bas-relief a base relief. And the family deranges the range with trilingual jokes, quelle est la matière, raped carrots, what is loose, have a good Fahrt, there is no what, taking something mit, grandpère a été délayé, like a sauce.

Geography consists of a straight coast sloping down westwards, Belgium humped behind like a headless hamster, cut into strips to be learnt: la zône limoneuse, la zône calcaire, la zône ferrugineuse. The little girl transforms: la zône limonadeuse, la zône calamiteuse, la zône vertigineuse.

And today the old map of Europe learnt at school is resurging with vertiginously calamitous zones from under the leaden palimpsest, not to mention the old map of Africa, ah, le Congo belge so proudly thrust into the children's imagination with jerky films at the Musée Colonial of black-breasted women pounding meal and savagely garbed black men stamping out war-dances in happy honour of the white chiefs.

Once upon a time there is a little girl born in French, of an English father and a Swiss mother born of an American father and an Anglo-Swiss mother. The English father lives in London, the American-Swiss mother in Geneva, with the now Swiss grandpère and the Anglo-Swiss grand'mère. That's the first split. Très wagon-lit, as Ian the joker, a brief wartime husband, says.

Back to London, back to Geneva, back to London, back to Brussels, back to back. Forgetting French, forgetting English, relearning French, relearning English, learning Flemish, learning German, forgetting Flemish, relearning English not really forgotten. Etc. That's the thirteenth split or so, scatterings and smatterings, French kindergarten in Geneva where the little girl at three stands on a stool by the Christmas tree reciting *Maman tire les rideaux*. English kindergarten in Brussels at four where the little girl and sister Joanne learn reading and multiplication tables in English singsong, and steal roses, hidden in elasticated knickers of pink cretonne, pregnant and prickly. At five a brown-uniformed day-school in Chiswick, Brussels and the kindergarten again, at six a blue-uniformed school in Chiswick. And mysteriously, to cover the transition back to Brussels, a brief governess called Miss Enoch, with an atlas. Joanne remarks triumphantly, France is bigger than England. The little girl looks and sees a sort of solid square for France and, for England, a crotchety old lady backside to the continent with stretched legs driving a motorcar into the Atlantic, Ireland as the wheel. But Miss Enoch turns to the world page and says Look, everything pink on the map belongs to England. The little girl looks at the dot of England and the huge expanses of pink and asks, Why?

What was the answer? says John[13] (John the litcritter).

Can't remember. An answer to how, probably. Quenching an infant's inkling about grown-up worlds about to vanish?

Pseudo-memory, more probably.

Sometimes the old lady hates John for the things John can't do, elapse.

Bifografy is always part fiction, John continues. First in the singulative birth, then in the iterative background, then in the singulative splits. Incoherent inchoative, incognitially punctuated. A situation, an event, another situation. Hero meets donor, is tested, receives a magical auxiliary, brains for instance or an eagle, is translocated to fight this or that dragon and returns incognito to perform another impossible task like emptying a river with a sieve, for recognition, then the whole cycle can start again and does, the recognition of desire being the desire of recognition (Lack-on). Pretty redundant, eh?

Pretty how?

Redundant.

Yes. A joke. Sorry. But girls in fairy-tales are never heroes, girls must be either Cinderellas or marry the prince, girls are a statue, a tower-prisoner, a block of ice, a pillar of salt, a deep sleep until a man comes along. Fogs lift, John, other fogs rise. People are fogs, fogs of experience, of talent, of knowledge. Each separating intelligence from talent, content from form, thought from feeling (etc). Neither men nor mentors can endure otherness. Oxford or Cambridge? the girls at the blue school ask, about some unheard of boat race. Well, choose a rosette, pale blue or dark blue? Pale blue. But daddy is not pleased with the pale blue rosette. Daddy went to Oxford. This turns out, many years later, to have been one of many fictions.

Why does talent belong to others?

In Brussels, asked the usual question about wanting to be what when grown-up: un écrivain. Guffaws. Joanne, oui, Jean-Luc, oui, there's imagination. Talent belongs to others, brains to the little girl. That seems very fair, brains at school and the inner games at home, for a quiet mouse. Yet on that day the little girl becomes a writer, Joanne and Jean-Luc never do. Or perhaps John is the writer, John a whole language, or more, a worldword memory. Or perhaps later, the sixteen-year-old girl whispering down a rabbit-hole on the Sussex Downs soon after the declaration of war: Hear O earth, a future writer, this is a solemn vow. The earth is very old and may have smiled benignly. Or guffawed malignly. But the girl hears only silent approval and awe, for the first great novel in the head, to be called Europe Street, each house representing a country, never of course written. That's the twenty-ninth split.

What does 'that' refer to?

Anything, the hole, the earth, the vow, the unwritten novel. Other splits are wrenched school friendships now forgotten, passions of intense brevity. The mentors, coming and going.

Mentors are sometimes tormentors, says John, imposing to destroy, creating a pigmylion illusion of structure, preferring to ignore rather than absorb another.

Tor-mentors, that's good, the old lady says kindly. For mentors are sometimes mentowers, usually alas dead, or imagined, Athene to Odysseus, for the first Mentor was a goddess, Homer to Virgil, Virgil and beady Beatrice to Dante, Dante to Pound and innumerable other strands, infinitely interwoven and sometimes shredded into –

Litter richer, says John flatly. The rat race. The mousetrap in the House of Fame or Fiction. John IS built by the House, flying reputations can be dangerous. Great, great, great, on cold grey stones of seachange, Stock Exchange, The Dow Jones Index of

Authors closing at minus seven and a half tonight. Masterpieces, and occasionally mistresspieces, pieces of author, morceaux choisis in infinite morsels of the body politic of litter rats.

John, being stylistically guileless, is not eager to please, nor eagle neither.

All writing, all work, says the old lady primly, is necessarily a piece of master, a piecemeal attempt to master a file, a life. Alter ego et galore.

Yes, says John, ignoring the anagram, in the lie-prairies a million straws lie trampled by the tractors of intractability, how's that for paronomasia, snarls John[13], stung at being called stylistically guileless, to be rounded up in rectangular packages like books and bundled out by the inexorable combine-harvester, stacked in scattered yellow groups of miniature skyscrapers, isolated remnants of cities regimented along the fields, fodder for beasts, the grain thrashed out by the inexorable machine and stored away in braineries elsewhere, in universities perhaps. Before the traitors came the bundles were forked up by hand and tied together in steeple-shapes, rows and rows of golden chapels more haphazard over meadows. How's that for imagery?

John[13] is eager but not easy to please, nor will John quite elapse.

There are so many others to confront, the credits rolling up the screen after the telefilm, the art director, casting adviser, location manager, script consultant, continuity girl, camera supervisor, focus-puller (*puller?*), director of photography, production assistant, composer, floor-manager, prop buyer, graphics designer, costume designer, make-up consultant (but everything is made up), lighting engineer, executive producer, director, and innumerable others contributing to the life remade, alter ego et galore, the old lady can't help repeating, for a laugh, a smile, in vain, all the mentors and all the selves, the baby in Geneva, the little girl in Chiswick, in Brussels, Folkestone, the young girl in Liverpool, in Thornaby-on-Tees, in Bletchley Park, in Occupied Germany, the student in Oxford, in London, the young wife and writer in Chelsea, the traveller in Spain, Austria, Italy, Eastern Europe, Turkey, the less young wife and writer in Hampstead, the middle-aged professor in Paris, in New York, Buffalo, Brandeis, Jerusalem, Geneva, Zurich, the old lady in Provence.

2. FILE

The old lady is watching a film about a writer on a rarer and rarer book-programme. The writer must be shown walking, in a garden, a city street, a park, and is, on Hampstead Heath. Walking solely for the camera, thinking. Not of words and work, but probably of the walk solely for the camera. The writer must be shown writing, a manuscript, the camera closeup on the pen, or at a typewriter, typing, surrounded with books and whisky, or at a word-processor, and is. The writer taps away. The little screen is shown on the big screen, with a text. Clearly the writer has been typing nothing on an unswitched processor, looking constantly from keyboard to empty screen. Separately the writer has put in the diskette of the book to show the text on the little screen, and called up visualized paras, returns and instruction windows to remake the tapping alive. The producer has toanfroed from the empty tapping to the text on the little screen. But the text is the text of the book presented in the film on the bigger screen, already published and distributed at the time of filming. That's creativity.

The old lady's fingers tap on the keyboard of erased memories, dead memories, retrievable memories, buffer memories, although John the script consultant is so much easier, eagerer to invent. Zapping between how many channels? With how many strange loops? With how much peur du grand méchant loop? Or let the best man win et que le méchant loupe.

The phrase century-so-almost-spanned conveys only public events, restories history not story, the parloir or parlourtricks of politics having solved nothing, not poverty, not unemployment, not the strata-strifes or frontier-feuds or deep intolerances, the imposed solutions exp(l)osed, the utopias like mentowers crashed

14

into entropias, every downfall a comeuppance, fascism defeated now back, the colonized freed only to corrupted dictatorships or to be recolonised into the inner cities of the old colonisers, displaced persons on the roads or in camps again or on the seas in small boats, discovering the dishonesties of dream demockeracy in a renewed Ost-racism, even antifascism anagrammed into fanaticisms, old time iconomies merely shifting names, flags, mental representations and other candyfloss symbols, the slump of the thirties solved by war for ever and now back but called recession, even the religious wars, turned ideological for several centuries now hotly religious again, power-driven either way, the planet retribalized, everyone behaving as to the manna born, in a crime-honoured way, castrating problems with Occam's razor, though careless reading costs lives.

An old Bosnian woman in a wheelbarrow, pushed by the family ethnically cleansed out. How can a badminton childhood or mere old age compare to that? But death is for other cultures, everyone so vocal as to be equivocal among interlocutors, each summit reached revealing another summit beyond another hollow. A badminton childhood compared to that is a bored storyboard.

A life, a human life? The Israelis always demanded the life of one Israeli hostage against 174 or so Palestinians, and the Palestinians, apparently seeing a bargain rather than a profound insult, always accepted.

Life versus history, Pasternak said, exclaims John the méchant loop angrily. First World lives worth more than others. Goulags, genocides, massacres, provoked famines, ignorance and poverty-bred epidemics, mass unemployment as a price worth paying, all still subliminally treated as lost spermatozoa, unhatched eggs, newborn turtles not reaching the sea, culture disguised as nature. Is that the meaning of the Church on natural birth-control? To be met by distress and prayer. Let others do the killing, institutions will do the deploring, high on ceremony and rhetoric but low on action, all munching away, setting up watchdogs and phantom tribunals for crimes against humanity, as if empty threats and appeals for diplomacy, peace, democracy, fairness, honesty had weight when criminal human groups clearly do not want these things, as in the thirties, the only way out, as in the thirties and as subliminally, being all out war, biological this time, accessible to all, and all the simplified old war-rhetoric can be flashed out again at a finger-flick.

Simmer down, John, this is yaquà café talk, elapse.

In this long span of misery resulting from the century's parlour-tricks, dogmatricks and polempic games the old lady can't decide, imagine, invent, select the life-file to call up first, if at all, even if re-treated as something else, inputting the databank of culture, attaching personal experience to collectivities, great events, significant mutations, at least as memory-joggers. But is that how experience was lived?

On 16 January 1923, third floor of 7 rue Lévrier Genève, the new baby pushes through blood and placenta face first all crumpled in cramped curiosity to see the world. Mummy is disgusted, thinks the crumpled face will remain so for ever.

Pseudo-memory, says John[32], the pedantic John.

BUT waking in terror eyes tight shut and screaming, Joanne screaming too in joint fear, grand'mère gently bathing the eyelids, l'homme de sable, chérie, no harm done. There's a distant clinking of bells early one morning, the little girls are held at the window to watch the mountain goats invading rue Lévrier way down below, the goat-herd selling cheese. Or to wave ava to grandpère walking off to work at the Librairie Naville. Maman also works, in the Bureau International du Travail, where the lifts move slowly but never stop, so jumping quickly in and out is essential. No, this was told later, oh shut up John. Stray shards forming into a nonsensical causal narrative: grandpère walking among the goats and maman jumping in and out of lifts just beyond the goats as the little girl waves with eyes tight shut. The Pont du Mont Blanc stretches huge and white and endless against a white city, a silver-white lake, white mountains, maman is pregnant and falls into a worker's hole creating fear for the future baby's life. But the future baby is Joanne, over a year before the little girl even exists as a cell.

So why part of memory? And the holidays in the Vallais, chez tante Dora at Ciergnat, where the little girl and cousin Daniel one day pack food in large handkerchiefs and vanish into adventure, or in winter fly down the mountain road on one toboggan while maman skis and Joanne wants to and wails? Or at Vaudagne, in the old family chalet near Chamonix, is that a memory or photographs, or two primitivist paintings on wood, now on the old lady's bedroom wall, by some American lady, of the two little girls among abundant and detailed flowers against an unusually visible Mont Blanc, all superimposed by later visits? Joanne falls from the balcony and yells for hours, but when the doctor comes gets up and runs away. No, that too is heard later, part of the Joanne-lore.

In 1948 the young woman of twenty-five visits Geneva with Janek. The Pont du Mont Blanc is as shrunk as the minds of aunts and uncles, the lake is grey, the mountains are invisible. Janek insists on seeing rue Lévrier 7 and kneels in hommage on the pavement. Janek is fond of picturesque gestures. Exactly twenty years later the image is repeated by chance in a side street near Henekey's Winebar, Janek kneels in hommage before Fiona standing against the low green MG in a pink Chanel suit and sleek but huge black hair. The young middle-aged wife in mid marriage-crisis slips away. But keeps seeing the couple, for Janek chooses shared old haunts, Henekey's, Regent's Park, Hampstead, as if wanting to be seen. Suddenly Fiona's green MG is there, parked for petting in Lower Hampstead after the regulation two nights away together. The wife drives past but gets caught in the small one-way streets and has to reenter the same road. The weekend farewells are over and Janek is walking away towards the car, Fiona is waving. On a wicked impulse the wife stops and offers Janek a lift up the hill, waving back at Fiona on the way past. Fury, accusations of spying and lying, though Janek has been lying steadily for months. Fiona was very upset, Janek says the next evening.

Personne n'a le droit d'être heureux tout seul, some Frenchman said. The old lady can't think of the name, but with a lifetime of scholarship behind, why check and hunt? Let the French source hop sit in the head, Sartre perhaps, never alone and needing women around to the last. Yet many beings are happy alone, thrust into or choosing solitude with mentors toppled by early death, by later desire or by inadequacy. Solitude is not loneliness. Don't such solitudinous persons have the right to be at least serene?

But then, can stimulus for confrontation of all those fogs come out of mere serenity, for undoubtedly the old lady is serene, rather than out of ruthless hurt thru and thru?

The old lady has already watched the even older, Tante Vanna for instance, remember the same youthful anecdotes over and over, but not the water boiling or the details of yesterday, all yesterdays shrunk to a small routine. Like soap's slices of life skewered on a shish-kebab, like thisful winking, like sentences embedded into a wonky recursive structure, like getting the memory of an elephant to crack a nut in a china-shop with a sonic stirrer, like a modern composer taking a syllable, a kettle's whistle to expand and cut up on a synthesizer. And now the old lady's yesterdays are going the same syllabic way.

But how far back to go?

The old lady's mind quantums off again. How far back in history can a nation go to settle frontiers of identity? To the Garden of Eden, to the Ur-text of Ur, to a Mosaic of ilk and money? To a Pilated colony, an Islamic conquest, a manly mandate, a diaspora, a shoa? Or to an idea incarnadined in the language of a treaty, the language of machine-guns (tak-tak)? Collective memory seems to be fabricated at school, on models ordered from above. The British Empire, l'Algérie française, la République, America land of the free, Et chantons en choeur le pays roman, Là-haut sur la montagne, Flamands wallons tous les belges sont frères, le belge sortant du tambour and all the rest.

Flying planes of meaning can be dangerous. Memesis. The Story So Far. But how far back to go?

Many egos ago. The old lady titters on the brink. Sitting in the garden under the pergola in the heat of July to the hysterical cicadas, leafing through a foolscap-size document bound in stiff grey paper, privately printed in Geneva. *Chronique de la famille Blair*. By Francis Blair, Oncle Francis, hardly a scholar and filling in early gaps with potted history, but verbose on the last generation.

File: the Blairs of Maryland. Robert Blair, born 1602 in Whitchurch Hampshire England, of Thomas and Susan Blair, a Catholic family, though Robert becomes an Anglican for a time as Rector of Wickham and Bible Clerk at Wadham College Oxford. In 1625 Robert meets Cecilius Calvert, later second Lord Baltimore, son of George Calvert, a Catholic convert. Both sail for Maryland as Catholics – these are turncoat times – and Robert Blair becomes governor of a newly created County Calvert along the river Patuxent, building De Blair Manor on the East side and Blair Place Manor on the West. The descendants lose these to a senior branch and the Blairs scatter all over Maryland (Blairfield, Blairville, Blair Court...). All respectable reverends and governors and judges, until Hunter Blair, the old lady's great-grandfather, a lawyer in Cincinatti and president of the Council, brilliant and popular but dissolute, at twenty-six meets Fanny Livingstone Butler, a girl of sixteen. Fanny, as the amateurish chronicle puts it, falls radically in love and, against the Butlers' wishes, marries the dashing Hunter Blair. Then everything changes.

For the couple is not happy. The Butlers, the flat narrative goes on, take Fanny back for a while, but a reconciliation is arranged and the Blair pair settles in Williamsport Pennsylvania, where Fanny founds some sort of music school. In 1858 a girl, Louisa, is born in great pain (how does Oncle Francis know?). Then in 1861 the Civil War breaks out and Hunter Blair enrols as private soldier in the 2nd Infantry regiment of Minnesota. On 10th December Fanny gives birth to a boy, George Warder Blair, again in great pain. Grandpère. Oncle Francis's father.

Well, yes, George Warder may be the son of Hunter. Hunter may not have left Williamsport until May. But Fanny, now twenty-two, runs off with the children to mum and dad, and the Butlers send back the first child Louisa to the Blair grandparents. The Reverend Butler, named in Rome, takes daughter Fanny and little George along and sends Fanny to a family in Vevey to recover. Fanny is now twenty-three, speaks three languages and is an accomplished pianist. Kept short of funds by the Butlers, Fanny gives lessons, then accepts a place as companion to a Russian lady in Geneva, Madame Tchibitchev.

There in 1863 Fanny meets a German Baron von Bodenhausen.

The Baron falls as radically in love as Fanny fell for Hunter. Fanny returns to America with little George in 1864, the Baron in hot pursuit. A divorce is obtained from Hunter, now returned as Colonel from the war and imprisonment in the South. Hunter is dallying, drinking and dilapidating the Blair fortune rapidly. The Baron marries Fanny in Bridgeport Connecticut and takes the bride home to the Rhineland, where the von Bodenhausen family does not welcome this dashing, dowerless, difficult American girl, nor does the difficult American girl take to the austere and rule-bound ways of the German small aristocracy. Other children come so George is brought up with German stepbrothers, but doesn't discover this, or the name of Blair, until the age of ten, with a shock, as noted much later in background notes written for future in-laws. Fanny starts travelling around in the entourage of Franz Liszt. Soon the Baron refuses to see either mother or son again and young George is sent en pension to Geneva.

So this is the fortuitous link between the Blair family and that mountainously boring city. The old lady has never felt particularly Swiss.

What Fanny does after that is unknown. The Baron pays a generous allowance for George's upbringing. Fanny comes to Geneva for George's wedding to a Swiss girl, Laure Paturin, a banker's daughter with an English mother, in 1888, when a birth-certificate for George is drawn up by an American attorney testifying how according to the sworn statement of the doctor attending the birth, George was born on 10th December 1862. The narrative says grandpère later maintains Fanny took a year off to seem younger.

Fanny Butler, the only interesting person in the family, dies obscurely in Bossum, Holland, in 1903. Called Grand-Maman Bono, for Bodenhausen, by George's children but otherwise barely known. On hearing of the death George hardly hurries, setting off on a bicycle.

The old lady and cousin Jean-Luc, at a reunion in Brussels after forty years, some sixteen years ago, to celebrate the eightieth birthday of Oncle Francis, look together at the awkward evasiveness of the *Chronique* and wonder with a good laugh whether grandpère and the European Blairs are not, say, Vanderbilts.

Why did the Butlers send Louisa back to the Blairs and keep little George? In those days, would a man separating from a wife keep the daughter and let the son go, unless not a son? But then, Hunter the dallier does not keep the daughter. Louisa is brought up by the Blair grandparents, so perhaps Hunter couldn't be bothered with either.

Even so, the photographs are strangely unlike. Hunter Blair at thirty-three has a long narrow face with down-slanted spaniel eyes, pouched, colour unknown but apparently dark, under thick eyelids and oblique half-eyebrows, like Louisa's, a long narrow nose, like Louisa's, a pursed weak mouth, like Louisa's, though half hidden in a fuzzy moustache, and thick frizzwavy hair, like Louisa's. Altogether a wet bedraggled look (wet because a soak?). Not a single Blair descendant looks like that, for George at about the same age is square-browed and jawed, has straight unpouched blue eyes under full straight eyebrows, the mouth is wide and firm, under a splendid sleek moustache, the hair is straight. Only the high broad brows seem vaguely akin, though Hunter's is narrower, and the noses, though Hunter's is longer and down-pointing, George's broad and aquiline. The Butler nose, sticking out on the still demure photograph of Fanny at fortyish, circa 1880, and on the profile medaillon sculpted by George in 1885.

There are no male descendants left, says Oncle Francis during a visit to the middle-aged lady, then fifty-six, in Paris, in the late seventies. Except, of course – Oncle Francis is nearly eighty and smirks. Oncle Francis has fathered one son, Jean-Luc, and Jean-Luc has three sons and four grandchildren, three male. Posterity is safe. The name Blair will survive. The middle-aged lady, having kept the name Blair-Hayley after marrying an unpronounceable Pole, has written many books and asks timidly whether these too might not also carry on the name, if only in library catalogues? After all, male descendance can die, as the *Chronique* shows. Oncle Francis stares at the middle-aged niece out of another world.

But isn't this obsessive pride in such an ordinary name a bit suspect? Grandpère made a collection of some 300 envelopes, 300 ways of misspelling Blair (Blaire, Belair, Blère, Blare, Blire, Bliar, Bliard, Blarie, Bière, Boire, Blois...) and had a genealogical chart worked out tracing the Blair family, as genea-illogical charts will, back through at least seven female lines to Charlemagne, female names, suddenly useful here, more normally disappearing. Could George have had some swamped inkling? People can be careless with inklings.

And Oncle Francis spent many retirement years researching and compiling the *Chronique de la famille Blair*, recording all the details, and yet, in pride at having generated the only remaining male Blairs, seems blind to other readings. Undeicidable.

George and Laure have six children, all dead now: a boy Walter, marries Swiss and has a daughter Josette, and a son with two daughters. Then four girls. The eldest, Alice, leaves for America at seventeen, furious at having to become Swiss like papa, when born American, and stays there, late-marrying American, no children; mummy, called Jeanne, marries an English roué Alfred Hayley, two daughters; Vanna, a eurhythmics dancer and teacher, marries a French diplomat, no children; Dora marries a Swiss pasteur, brother of the big bookseller Librairie Naville and has a son, Daniel, remarries a pasteur after being widowed and has three daughters. And, last of the six, Francis, marries Swiss and continues the Blair line in Brussels. Four of the six, Walter, Alice, Jeanne and Dora, have the Paturin brown eyes and the round Paturin nose, only Vanna and Francis (and the old lady, a throwback), take after grandpère, with the blue Butler eyes and the strong Butler nose.

The old lady, like a child with a changeling fantasy, still likes to think of the real descendance as not Blair at all but Vanderbilt. Or Rockefeller.

Tante Vanna, or Giovanna, Jeanne's favourite sister. The two names are the same, in different languages, grandpère's little joke. The two girls, Jeanne brown-eyed and Vanna blue-eyed, are in the middle of the four, played together when not playing all four at *Little Women*, Jeanne as Jo of course, Vanna as Amy. Vanna is less intelligent than Jeanne but prettier, just as Alice is less brilliant than Walter but more hard-working. On such parentities are futures built. Jeanne, though as pretty as the others, feels ugly, meets Alfred Hayley, forty-three and divorced without saying so, in New York at the end of La Grande Guerre.

Jeanne is twenty-five and in love with a young but married Californian painter, joins the Red Cross and flees to war-torn Europe with Alfred in pursuit as ardently as the baron had pursued Fanny the other way in 1864, and then to Geneva after the Armistice, kabaled by Laure into the arms of this feckless old Englishman of great pretensions, so much better than a young but married Californian painter. And Jeanne perhaps is even grateful, ignorant of the miseries to follow, escaping later into the arms of the Catholic Church and later still, after the Second War, into the arms of a Benedictine Order as a nun. At fifty-two. A late vocation.

Tante Vanna, studied then taught eurhythmics with Jacques Dalcroze, inventor of that then new discipline, composer of songs the whole family knew and passed on, singing à deux voix. Star-pupil of the troop doing demonstrations in Russia, Poland, Germany, then married a grumpy French minor diplomat, living first in Paris then Stockholm, then after the war in Angola and Sicily. Oncle André refuses to have children, hence Vanna's tendency to meddling love for nephews and nieces. Photographs of Vanna's graceful gestures in a Greek tunic.

Tante Vanna: a late second mother, as a widowed old lady in Grasse with a memory shrivelled to familore: Francis as a little boy on seeing the postman in civvies says le facteur déguisé en homme. Dora said, Jeanne did, maman, that is, grand'mère – oui, raconte, why did the family move to Brussels?

A scandal. Several scandals. Laure Paturin now Blair has the spending sickness, ordering on credit dozens of sheets, table-cloths, dishes, clothes for the children and constant gifts. Not selfishly, not wildly, keeping rigorous accounts, revealed when the tradesmen complain. The first time, in 1899, is hushed up with the banker father's help, the second time can't be as the banker father is dead and papa – grandpère – has to sell the house in Florissant. Papa works for *Le Journal de Genève* and is successful but not rich. The move to the rue Voltaire is a catastrophe of snobshame for Laure, near the railway and worse, on the rive droite! The Paturin brothers and sisters all live in posher parts. Laure falls ill and is sent away to recover. In 1909, same drama. George sells a precious collection of etchings, publishes a refusal of responsibility, and Laure is given a guardian. George is now at home for meals only, goes out to dance in cabarets and leads, as the *Chronique* says, a dissolute life. This can hardly help.

The old lady looks at the chorus lines of long-limbed dancing vines, clear now in the evening sun. Time to go in from the pergola, get supper, watch the summer nonsense on TV. But no, even the flat narrative is better than the loud nonsense.

In 1916, new drama: Laure has been buying morphine since 1909 on credit from the pharmacist. A habit contracted at the first nursing-home. George wants to commit suicide, but doesn't. Laure is sent to a clinic in Kreuzlingen for a tough disintoxication.

All the offspring are away, the girls in America, except young Francis. Francis is told, exit Francis, shocked, to work in Basle for a few years, but ending up in Brussels and starting up a small travel agency in a tiny flat. This will become Les Voyages Blair, with branches all over Belgium, and still exists. For Francis sells up when retiring at seventy, on condition the name be kept. The famous, the ordinary name. Still over every branch, so much more visible than books.

But the eventual move of George and Laure to Brussels in 1926, to make a late new start, is not, contrary to Vanna's version, because of Laure, and this is a relief, for Laure after heroic efforts has truly recovered, even becomes the model of excess economy as remembered, teaching the little girl never to cut the string of parcels but to undo the knots, roll up the string, fold up the wrapping paper, and to keep every scrap of material – could be useful. And to take a different tea towel for glasses, plates, silver and saucepans, the cloths last longer that way, though privately the little girl feels one cloth changed four times as often would come to the same thing. Vanna has the same minimanias, easily enough obeyed. And when moving into the Old People's Home the emptying of drawers together is a slow torture, every scrap of stuff hesitantly held – could be useful.

No. The move to Brussels has occurred because George, working in the Librairie Naville, has compromised all reputation in some adventure, and at Monsieur Naville's request has to retire. George is sixty-five. Yet both become model grandparents as remembered.

So Brussels is another chance connection, like Geneva. The old lady has never felt particularly Belgian either. No ancestral roots. Not even the Blairs of Whitchurch Hampshire England, only the Butlers of Pennsylvania, and perhaps some mythical Vanderfeller. Every place a foreign land.

In the mind of the old lady this drearilistic tale, though piecemealed from hearsay over many years and now reread on a mosquitoed July night, has nevertheless formed images. How can that be? Fanny pursuing Liszt from concert to concert, Hunter drinking dissolutely from a bottle labelled Blair Fortune, Jeanne a khaki clad Red Cross Nurse in a hospital at St Denis, Alfred Hayley pursuant on a ship writing desperate letters, Laure stabbing an arm, George galant at cafés-dansants, Francis selling railway-tickets in a mansard flat. Images as live as the remaining fragments of experienced life.

Such as the little girl at four, for instance, living in a tall narrow house with dark and darkly furnished rooms at 34 avenue Mahillon, Bruxelles, opposite a long brick wall hiding la caserne – a frightening word said in ominous tones. Addresses are always incrusted into the child's mind, maybe for brink-anchorage of precarious permanence, of belied belonging. For here is family, three families, grandpère and grand'mère, maman and Joanne, Oncle Francis and Tante Mathilde and Jean-Luc, blond and curly. And a Swiss au pair Vally. Grand'mère, warmly voluminous in floating black and grey, goes to the market behind la caserne, coming back laden with six shopping-bags, three on each side.

Jean-Luc at three cuts up worms, to show how each half continues alive, in the long strip of walled garden under the clustered mauve hydrangeas at the end, and climbs a pear-tree to the little girl's room, locked up for something or other Jean-Luc has done. The little girl always plays with Jean-Luc, never with Joanne, say under the tapestry-covered dining-room table, safe behind the walls of heavy cloth, playing Post Office with Jean-Luc's set. But every Sunday morning all three clamber up to grandpère's room at the top of the house to draw straight lines in exercise books, in case, perhaps, the children should become politicians drawing up frontiers and dividing cities. And the English kindergarten of the multiplication tables and prickly roses, run by four sisters, the

Misses Marx, far away in Uccle, Tess and Joanne taken and fetched by maman or grand'mère in butter-yellow trams. Jean-Luc doesn't go to school yet, or goes to a different kindergarten, not needing English immersion yet.

The images are as vivid and evanescent as those of the drearilistic story unlived except by hearsay, as vivid as Charlequint abdicating or Napoleon waiting for Grouchy and getting Blücher in the morne plaine, out of school text-books maybe.

Talking with grey-aired Vanna in the Grasse flat during the seventies, singing Dalcroze à deux voix during the washing up, playing French Scrabble, going into stitches at long words and old stories till both have to rush and pee. Sliding now into childhood but without Vanna, in Paris or Stockholm at the time, with visits to Brussels only part of Joanne's label The Well-Meaning Aunts, in earnest asides, maman a tant de peine, why can't the chère petite nièce be a clean little girl, like Joanne, why can't Joanne be quiet and helpful, like the little girl, why can't both be like Jean-Luc, so clever, so obedient? Jean-Luc by now going to an expensive private school.

Is the old lady going, at seventy, the same way as Vanna in early dotage?

3. FILE: PRO-NOUNS

Mummy's memory in old age, at the Benedictine convent, is quite unlike Vanna's, as if the new mentor Christ had made the world and previous life insignificant. At least till the very end.

The old lady sits at the computer in the study, in the heat of August, beside a ventilator, all windows and shutters closed, a Southern custom learnt the hard way after the first summer of foolishly open windows. But then gets up and starts searching the drawers under the books, in a sweat away from the ventilator, looking for a bit of diary kept at the time. The old lady is not a diary-keeper, or at least, any diary kept for a while by way of exercising English when not writing, became lazy and unreadable even the next day, and was thrown away: Got up early, slept badly, weather drizzly, difficult meeting, Jean-Pierre rang and talked for an hour. Despite such telegraphese, diaries are full of pronouns. Like this one, ah, here, not exactly a diary but a meditative account of a dying and a death, written between the acts.

July 1984, Südtyrol, Northern Italy, in the flat called the Green Grotto, because it has a small garden behind the parapet of the castle Brünnenburg, above Merano, where Ezra Pound's daughter Mary and her family live. My nose has been blocked since March, despite endless antihistamines creating colds to melt the blockage, in vain.

It is Friday, and a call comes at five from the Mother General. Mummy has had a stroke, can I come at once. I ask her, shall I travel via Geneva, and bring Joanne? No, she says, Joanne would upset her. I dither for two precious hours. Should I wait till tomorrow and fly? It means a taxi down to Merano, a train to Bolzano, another train to Milan or Venice or Munich and hanging around for a plane, all in intense heat and holiday crowds. At last I put all the food I have in the fridge into the car and leave for the Brenner Pass at seven. The evening becomes a bright moonlit night and I drive fast along the almost empty Autobahn as if by day. I stop in a Parkplatz and try to sleep for an hour but can't. Though I am calm. She will be ninety-two this month, after all.

Soon forty years as a nun. I remember the shock when she first went in, just after the war, at fifty-two. Visits are difficult at first, mummy's entry feels like death without the paraphernalia of death. I used to read that as paraphrenalia, as if from phreno-, mind, instead of pherna, dowry, or rather, chattels the wife is allowed to keep for herself over and above the real dowry brought to the husband. Therefore it now means trivia. Out of mind in a way.

I have never understood why women had to pay for the privilege of losing their freedom. In India, women in poverty abort or murder baby girls because of expensive rituals, up to and including the dowry, rather than abolish the rituals. Get rid of the paraphernalia, as Pound says Ino said to Odysseus.

I remember the fuss made by Tante Mathilde and Oncle Francis about mummy paying her share of a small inheritance from grandpère, held back by the war, to the convent as dowry. The Church of Rome is a money-grabber and so forth. Yet for that then largish sum of £800, mummy has been kept for forty years, if not in comfort, and not without much hard work, at least in calm security, a good investment to my irreligious eye. I know she thinks so too, but hushes me when I say it, in case the nuns overhear, or her divine husband perhaps. The nominally Protestant family finds mummy's decision difficult to understand, and Tante Dora, a practising Protestant twice married to pasteurs, can't remember the initials OSB, Order of St Benedict, to be added after the adopted name, and addresses envelopes Mother Mary Anselm, Deo Gratias, which delights us.

But I soon grow closer again to her. I too cut off much of the world, head in the clouds, though for different passions, the so-called higher things, God for her, thought-systems and other fictions for me. I know all the nuns, some of them mentally arrested at seventeen and giggling at all I say, others more mature and dignified. Serenity everywhere. But she is isolated in her God-routine. The most difficult hurdle at first is not the vow of poverty, even less the vow of chastity, nor the vow of obedience, but the recreation hour. Even in what the convent calls 'the world', other people were always a problem for her, she would look at them out of her velvety brown eyes and smile, unsure how to step out of her elsewhere or what to say, except banalities. She is isolated also in her tasks, prioress twice in the Sussex house, or in charge of the kitchens – the only time the nuns eat well, for I bring her seeds of French vegetables to plant in the garden – or the linen-room, mending the nuns' underwear or making and embroidering vestments, even quite late, when her eyes are failing. She talks of these things, and the life of prayer, and the reading she does, Saint John of the Cross, Saint Augustine, Saint Anselm. She talks of my career, proud of me at last. And of Joanne, so difficult: each time she tears up Joanne's aggressive letters in unchristian fury.

And as time passes she finds the world outside, the postwar (posthuman?) world, the world of her daughters, more and more alien, relating to it only in terms of her own past: Joanne keeps losing her jobs and never saves a penny, what will become of her? Quietly pleased with me, not, as I would like, at my study-mania but at my then Catholic leanings under her and Janek's influence, trying to get an annulment of my brief wartime marriage so that we may stop living in sin and marry before God. But then, when in mid marriage-crisis, way back in '68, I rush down to St Benedict's Priory in Sussex in a false back-to-mother impulse, she exclaims: Your father did it, your grandfather did it, all men are beasts, as if that were the problem rather than a symptom of other things. And later, after I tell her of the sudden job-offer from the University of Paris, she rings me in Hampstead by extraordinary permission (or was she Prioress then?) and tells me not to go. Why? Because if you get a job he won't support you. As if etc. If I had listened to her at every stage I would never have done anything. Back-to-mother means back to mother's forties and the century's thirties. And yet, yes, full of awkward tenderness and concern. And resigned forgiveness later when, free again, I return to my early twenties or even childhood and abandon all religion. But how forgiving was that forgiveness, how much did it cost her, how much a mere avoidance? For despite the acquired serenity

I remember how she half enjoyed drama, about the Other Woman, daddy's loss of faith, death, the declaration of war, my first divorce. But yes, it is possible, I reflect as I drive, to live in different worlds and still be close and full of love. As in different ways with Janek.

And then, in extreme old age, how well surrounded she is, looked after, bathed in love. And she has kept a few vanities: a few months before the stroke, she stages a coquettish, un-nunlike rebellion against the new wimple and tight round cap under it, which she refuses to wear, so ungainly, so plain. They humour her, because she is so old.

By eight I am circling Cologne towards Aachen and Liège, by lunchtime I am picnicking near Tournai, by three I'm on a ferry, by seven, eight for me, I arrive at Tyburn Convent in Hyde Park Place. Twenty-five hours of driving. But quicker, probably, and certainly cheaper and more tranquil, than trains and taxis and hanging around airports.

After being fed in the basement parlours I am taken into the consecrated part of the house to see her. A shock. That gentle face, framed after all in the new round white cap, is contorted, her soft brown eyes are as small as two flies in a faded flower, but glaring, vacant, staring at me from the bed. She is half paralysed on the left side. But she can hear me, and even answer yes or no. She's better than yesterday, they say.

I wake with a poison headache from the ham and salami rotted in the heat. I vomit but feel just as bad afterwards. Finally I ask for help as I can't see her in this nauseous state. The guest-mistress brings me hot peppermint and Panadol. It works. After lunch I talk to her again, much longer. My mother. The only person in the world who has known me all my life, sixty-one years, and yet has told me so little of it, or of hers.

Do you want to see Joanne?

No.

But her face is more relaxed, her mouth still twisted down, her beetle-eyes still glaring blankly, and she can't smile.

Are you at peace?

Yes.

Are you afraid?

No.

Do you want to get well?

Yes.

Do you feel close to God?

Hesitation, then, humbly and with effort: Sometimes.

I break down and cry, she looks at me, registering but unable to show emotion.

Mother Prioress, leading me back, says it's no use crying or worrying, it helps neither your mother nor you.

The nuns spoil me, bringing me Bovril in my room, it's all I can take, so I don't have to make conversation in the parlour dining-room with other guests and au pair girls. I hear on the radio that the dock-strike, which has so far spared holiday crowds, is going to close Dover altogether on Monday. I mustn't be stranded here. I decide to leave tomorrow. There's nothing I can do, she's in good hands.

I see her at eight, before leaving, and explain guiltily. She is legions away from such paraphernalia, but gives me a stare as I turn back at the door, clearly feeling she'll never see me again. Outside, I break down again. Where does all this emotion well from? I've been expecting this for some ten years.

The same journey in reverse. There should be windscreen wipers for eyes. Perhaps all this crying will unblock my nose. Back at the castle, Mary comforts me and gives me camomile, and I sleep soundly at last.

I ring London. She's not only better but the doctor thinks the left arm is not paralysed after all, merely broken in her fall, and the older femur-break has recurred. So they are sending her to St John's Hospital for X-rays, and if it's so they'll keep her there. Is this good news or not? She's well looked after in the convent, and will feel estranged in hospital, might die there among unknowns. But at least she's not paralysed.

Mary has helped me move into the flat below hers, now free, on the other side of the castle, overlooking the whole of the Adige valley. I watch the cars crawl like cockroaches along the narrow ribbons below, and the orange bus creep up to Turnstein, disappearing under woods for a long time then reappearing again on the last bend and stopping. The mountains slowly darken with solidity against the setting sun, but others behind them are almost frail and flimsy, like aluminium cut-outs. Later St Peter's church is lit up in amber on the slope, and Schloss Tyrol in ghostly white against the black mountain. Calm has returned, as if at the bidding of Mother Prioress.

Vanna writes me trivial letters from her Old People's Home, full of details about her small routine, and bitterly reproaching me for my cruelty in spending so short a time with her on my way to Italy. She hasn't long to live, she says, why doesn't God call her? She is now totally deaf and going blind, it's hard to communicate, and she too has forgotten the outside world, or what a huge detour it is for me to go to Merano from Paris via Grasse, or how expensive now that she no longer has her flat. Both my mothers are on their way, and the coming wrench is heightened by the witnessing of these degenerations, each one so different.

End of September, Monday, just before going off to teach for a term in Zurich. I've come to London again. The gloomy basement parlours in Tyburn are freezing as usual, despite the warmth outside.

She is still a crumpled old woman, but her features have relaxed, the angry glare of the stroke is gone, and her speech has returned. Though she is very confused. When I talk of Vanna she thinks I'm talking of Joanne, because I explain, for conversation, that I'm having to help Vanna out financially as the fees of the Home have gone up. A confusion of sisters, hers and mine, linked by penury in her mind. She wants to know if we're living together in the Anchorhold, the much smarter guest-flat of the Sussex house, where she was before.

No, I'm in London.

Oh. But is Joanne at the Anchorhold?

No, she's in Geneva.

Oh. Geneva... You must tell her, she must ask for an old-age pension here. She has saved nothing.

But mummy, she's now a Swiss citizen. She has a job, and will get a pension there.

Oh. There.

Do you want to see Joanne?

Yes.

But when I ask Mother General she tells me to take no notice. Your mother doesn't know what she's saying, tomorrow she won't remember, and won't understand what Joanne is doing here. When Mother Prioress told her you were coming she said oh, I thought she was here already. I have to publish her, she said.

It's true I have a book coming out.

Mother General said mummy's gently going down, won't get any better. But I now decide to ask Mother Prioress to insist with Mother General. Mummy has said yes, and that's enough for me.

Her confusion is more moving than Vanna's self-centred pettiness. I'm having a wonderful time, she says, watching the tree in the garden. I prefer nature to people.

I have to go to the BBC for an interview. After supper I see her again. She is in pain from her left leg, and bedsores, though it's a water-mattress.

Who was with you at the party last night with Joanne? And why are you talking so funnily?

I tell her about my nose, still blocked, I'm to see the doctor again in Paris.

Well, the doctor is downstairs, he's working with you, reading book-reviews.

How do the elements get connected? It sounds like dreams. I'm not very good at coping. Instead of humouring her, prolonging the small fictions, I'm afraid, and either deny – there was no party, my book isn't out yet so there can't be reviews, to which she replies that they must be reading their own reviews – or I let it go and after a silence say something else. I must try the other method.

On the way back to the parlours Mother Prioress tells me she has spoken to Mother General and Joanne can be sent for after all. The nuns have never liked Joanne, who tended to hire a taxi from Gatwick all the way to Wadhurst and arrive with whisky and fine clothes, criticize everything then say she's too poor to pay for her stay. So I ring Joanne in Geneva, offer to pay her fare. She's coming Saturday.

I can see people in the tree outside, mummy tells me on Wednesday. Lots of them, Horchst and Emma, from Hahnsdorf, you remember Hahnsdorf? She thinks I'm Vanna. What was the name of the eldest? And they're eating each other.

Is it a mystical eating, like the Sacrament?

No. One of them is Piglet. I haven't slept at all well.

Mother Assunta, the guest-mistress, comes for me. Joanne has rung, will ring again in exactly ten minutes and wants me to be by the phone in the parlour hall. Why didn't you say twenty, Mother? She laughs gently. My dear, your sister gives her marching orders and not a second for me to say anything.

So I go back to the parlours. Mummy has no idea of time. Joanne is coming on a cheap flight Friday and indignantly rejects my offer of her fare, but I can pay for her stay at the convent, it'll save her a hotel. I go to a huge luncheon party at Bertorelli's, given in my honour by my publisher. I see her again at five, for the first time ever without her wimple cap. Her thin white hair is clipped short, her face suddenly looks like a boy's, instead of an old woman's. She keeps her eyes closed. I'm dead, she says. I can't understand why they keep trying to feed me.

But mummy, you must eat.

I asked for fruit and they brought me an apple. It was nice. How did you get on at the BBC?

So she is partly aware, if slowly.

I go to Compline.

I'm in a box, she says on the next visit.

What box?

The coffin.

Are you afraid?

No.

Joanne is coming tomorrow.

Has she been published? Is she still writing?

No, that's me. Will you want to see her alone?

Oh yes, I'd better see her alone. Or maybe with you, together.

Fine.

Isn't it difficult for you to come so far, with all those people dangling their legs? I'm taking so long dying.

She's excruciatingly uncomfortable. Lying on a bag of nuts, she says. They're always poking and turning and hurting me.

They don't mean to.

The little man praying there in the corner is going to fall off.

Well, it's better to fall off while praying than while not praying.

She smiles.

All those people there, are they penitents?

They're probably pilgrims.

How did you come over the balustrade?

We climbed over and they brought us through.

In advance, I include Joanne. It's only a fiction after all. I put the flowers I was given at the luncheon in a vase for her.

On Friday I walk across Hyde Park to have coffee with Jean Bradley, née Stelling, of Bletchley Park warwork, and she talks of that.

Back at twelve. Joanne has arrived. Well-dressed as usual, though she's thickened a bit more than I have so far, her grey hair short and naturally curly, her grey eyes still glaring out of her narrow face. It goes surprisingly well. She still interrupts and doesn't listen and booms on in her deep voice, or waits for me to finish the word-in-edgeways before going on with her thing. Apart from aggressive letters I've never existed for her face to face, except as a wall to talk at, and my urge to answer those letters is a foolish attempt to be, rather than be abolished. But she's making an effort. There's no dragging up of old accusations. We even talk normally in the big parlour, full of junk furniture and with its windows on to Hyde Park glazed over. I ask her aren't you glad you worked in so many countries unvisitable now, like the Lebanon, Ethiopia, Irak? And she agrees enthusiastically, glad to be able to extol her way of life. She expresses surprise that the nuns wanted her here at all, and I stupidly say they didn't at first, but I insisted, thinking even more stupidly that she might be pleased. One should never give any item of information to Joanne.

Luckily she lets it pass. With mummy, she's admirable, better than me, talking of rabbits in Brussels (*rabbits?*), of Geneva and going up the Salève, producing a glossy magazine published by her firm, for which she has done the captions, and showing her the photographs as to a child. She talks in French and is answered in French. Mummy seems to light up when hearing about Geneva and mentions Florissant. Joanne gives her a small radio and she

35

examines it like a toy as we slip away. Mother Edmund Campion doesn't think Mother General will allow the radio, but Mother General floats along the polished corridor, and does. In the evening Joanne sees her alone.

At supper Mother Prioress half lets it out in front of Joanne that the stroke happened in July, but I cover up quickly, though Joanne gives us one of her frightening, suspicious glares. Damn it, they imposed the lie on me by insisting I shouldn't send for her then, or even tell her, they might at least keep it up.

Back in Paris, I see the doctor, who removes a large slobby lump from my nose. What bliss, I can breathe again.

Zurich, nineteenth of December, evening. No more classes till after Christmas. Mother Prioress has rung. I'm to come at once. I leave early the next day, in the snow at first, but it's sunny in Alsace. I sleep two hours in my Paris flat, though I've lent it for that purpose to the Portuguese concierge for her two daughters as they sleep five in the tiny *loge*, but she was amazed by my offer and is my friend for ever. I push on at three a.m. I should have flown but have to go via Paris because of a Zurich inefficiency, they've lost a document they need and I have a copy in Paris. And driving soothes me.

They say she's more conscious, and says things that make sense, though not with me. Mother Prioress tells me she's more aware than one thinks. How does she know? Her stare has returned, but anguished, no longer angry, and she seems at moments to have no idea who I am.

You must come tomorrow, everyone will be there.

And later: Take it off... Don't take it off before four.

This is repeated like a litany, with variations: before three, until they're all there. Then for a while it becomes: it isn't ready to go. Followed after ten minutes by: please don't wipe their mouths until it's ready to go. Endlessly, like a prayer, and after a while: please don't mark their wipes until its ready to go.

Joanne has refused to come.

At last she's quiet, though coughing. She can't bring it up, so I suppose the lung will slowly choke. Her hand is icy, or else burning. She goes up and down, with temperatures up to 106. This physical resistance amazes them. They say she was always very strong, digging in the garden, working hard. As a young mother she was always exhausted.

Could she, after all, be resisting? Or do we all, however close to what we may or may not believe to be everlasting love and peace, cling desperately to life, however painful?

At nine thirty in the evening they fetch me. The nuns are kneeling round the bed, holding lit candles and saying endless rosaries and Salve Reginas. She is in quick laboured breathing. Mother General kneels near her, wiping her mouth and nose with kleenex as she ave-marias. Then I take over the wiping. I'm holding her head which is falling sideways, then pull the pillow round to support it. At eleven forty her breathing slows down, and down, at larger intervals. I ask permission to say the Ave Maria in French, but break down after the third and they take over in Latin again. At eleven fifty she dies quietly, a short while after one breath. I wait for the next and know it won't come, and bow my head as Mother General intones the Prayer for the Dead.

Now she does look peaceful, but the serenity of last moments seems not to have been for her. Or has it? They file out, leaving me alone with her for a moment. I kiss her suddenly waxen brow. Outside, I cry out wildly against the wall, wondering at such pain.

Mother Prioress takes me back to the parlours. She asks me if I should or she should inform Joanne. Please Mother, you do it. She tells me she has received a nine-page letter from Joanne, which she couldn't read. I know those long typed letters only too well.

The Requiem Mass is the next day, in the Chapel. As if death had been planned ahead. But no, old Mother Magdalena died two days ago. I knew it but had forgotten, all to my own sorrow. The undertakers are willing to do two funerals together. Irrationally I feel it's unfair not to give her one of her own. But it's very beautiful, with the nuns singing in the choir, clad in ivory stoles over the black habit, but only partly visible, the public chapel being at right angles to theirs, facing the side-view of the altar. I can see the two coffins. Before the Mass I was allowed to see her on the bed, all washed and dressed in her nun's habit, looking smaller, like a saint encased in glass. So that's what she meant when she said I must come tomorrow, everyone will be there.

Outside in Hyde Park Place there are two hearses. The Cardinal steps out to offer his condolences and I curtsy deeply and kiss his ring in tears, feeling a sham. Later I'm almost ill with heaving sobs and they put me to bed and bring me whisky, but I can't even bear the smell. They give me valium and I sleep a bit.

I make myself some tea. Mother Prioress comes in to talk. You're almost part of the community, she says. I start crying again. Why? I thought I'd done all my deep mourning in advance, it was all so expected. We used to talk in this very parlour, she sitting in this very armchair, as recently as last February.

Sunday is a long, dreadful day. The life of the convent continues. I go to Nones. I go to Vespers. I ring Vanna's Home and leave a message, then write her a long letter describing everything for her in huge letters. I calm down at last. But I've lost my only true friend. I've had two of that intimacy in my life, she and Janek, and I've lost them both.

On Monday I leave for St Benedict's Priory, near Wadhurst, where the burial takes place. All the nuns are buried at the end of the huge garden, in long little parallel mounds, each with a wooden cross. It's raining, and to my horror the open grave is water-logged. An old priest has come from Tunbridge Wells and reads out the prayers fast and loud and aggressively as if personally furious at God and death. I have no more tears, it's all too dreary, and bitterly cold. As soon as I can, before the burial of Mother Magdalena, I leave for Dover. In Paris I receive a six-page letter from Joanne, which starts:

How kind of you to have insisted – against everyone else's wishes – that I be summoned so's Mummy could see us both together, as I proposed to you, in writing, almost 2 years ago. Funny thing is that in a chat I had with the Ma P on arrival, she told me she'd done the insisting. Have since had 2 very nice letters from the Ma P. She understands about my not attending the funeral. So will Mummy, from Heaven or wherever. I considered it a matter of basic courtesy to tell the Ma P why nothing could have induced me to attend. But I also told her I would have no objection at all to her showing you my letter to that effect, nor to her getting your side of the sordid saga if she so desired.

Now I have some *news* for you.

Which consists as usual, among the old questions to be aggressed, the out and outrage, the abuse and upbraiding, of an equally old conviction that we were on the same wave-length up to our early thirties, until I spoilt it all single-handed by my upbraiding and by perpetually allotting myself the beau rôle, that old rigma-role. And posing as a sinny kwa for recapturing that wave-length, but on her terms, that I cease upbraiding.

My wave-length, if it ever existed, snapped at around sixteen. She may be part of my psyche but she has long ceased to be part of my life.

I reply briefly that I've tried for forty years to get on with her and help her whenever she asked, for mummy's sake, but now there's no point. For three years I receive her aggressions on déjàbusives postcards to make sure I'll read them. One of them would have me know that present status Q is entirely acceptable to her. And you could've spared yourself the inconvenience (or should I say the pleasure?) of penning some more abuse. And adds: The FINANCIAL TIMES crit didn't arf hit the nail bang on the head. As I had long suspected, the shit is a lot happier than the saint, and quite a bit saner too, it would now seem.

There are no Jamesian hyperhesitancies or convoluted subtleties about Joanne. I have long forgotten what the Financial Times said, but surely it wasn't anything like that. There has always been this invented rivalry about happiness. The Financial Times seems to be the latest version of friends who shall be nameless, or, once, a very unprofessional-sounding psychiatrist who implausibly agreed to read all my letters and equally implausibly echoed her exact view of me. Or even posterity, with a mad blackmail about keeping my letters in a bank vault. Since I threw hers away I'd be at a disadvantage if I believed in posterity. Could she be subscribing to a Press Cuttings agency just for this purpose? After a quarter of a century of publishing I know that anything uttered betrays the utterer, or at least is susceptible to interpretation other than what the utterer intended, such as a role, beau or not. But Joanne never seems to apply this to herself.

There have always been, too, these assurances that no-communication is entirely acceptable, always followed, à la proche

haine, by more communication, and indeed the postcards con-
tinue with repeated apologies for not sending a cassette record-
ing, never asked for, of her version, and then a prepared speech
by phone to say she's going into hospital and may not survive to
record the cassette goodbye, with not a second for a good luck.
But the cassette does eventually arrive.

The old lady has never opened even the envelope, and a few
years later retires to Provence, unlisted.

Vanna is now deaf, blind, and impotent, lifted from bed to
armchair and back, smelling of sour milk, waiting impatiently
for the food to arrive. The old lady visits regularly. But the last
two times is unrecognized, taken for the nurse, despite embraces
and caresses, asked if the catheter is well fixed. In November 1989
the Home rings. Vanna has died, in bed, alone.

Two sisters, deeply different but each other's favourites. Two
other sisters, deeply different, but from the first irreconcilable.

4. FILE: ALPHA BETA

Alpha beta gamma delta EPsilon, with a tickle on the tummy. The third rote alphabet. At daddy's knee in the dining-room, yes, Chiswick. The first alphabet is years behind in Geneva, the second in singsong at the Misses Marx in Brussels. And now at the brown school the two sisters at five and six write and read and do sums.

The little girl's name is Tess. Only a name and memory can tesselate and texture all those different beings, the baby in Geneva, the little girl in Brussels, Chiswick, Brussels, Folkestone, London, and all the others to the old lady in Provence.

Watching a documentary on the media about documentaries on the media, the remake of history through faked images, Lenin gesticulating to the future on a high stand cleansed of contemptuary surround, Dubcek and colleagues during the Prague Spring, later effaced, the ex-colleagues brought closer together, only the tip of Dubcek's shoe peering out behind a trouser-leg, unnoticed by the effacer. Memories can be invented. Things have got cleverer now, not truer.

Joanne and Tess, six and five, walk together along Acton Green in brown tunics and vyella shirts and brown ties under brown blazers and porkpie hats, to the brown school, a brown house in a side-street with a brown wooden porch. No notion then of taking kids to and from school by car for safety, nor did ordinary families have cars. Granny is here on a visit. Granny was grand'mère at l'avenue Mahillon, mummy was maman. Granny and mummy bring the new bicycles at four, surprise, and hold on as Tess and Joanne learn to ride in Acton Green. Granny is tubby with short wavy grey hair and wears flowing black and grey. No

41

grannies are like that any more, not even the childless old lady, wrinkled around the neck and mouth and eyes, the nose oddly bigger than on younger photographs, the eyes oddly smaller, the thick long eyelashes of youth, so often and oddly praised and touched by Joanne, now shorter and sparser, the owner a bit stiffened and thickened all round but otherwise swimming, walking, weeding. Though more and more having to pay for weeding, and always for ladder-jobs like cutting the roses on the pergola. Time is in the head, a question of period.

Daddy leaves every day by the Underground, overground here, taking the Green Line to the city. The Green Line must be because of Acton Green and Turnham Green. The city is mysterious. Why does daddy go there? To the office, darling.

Tess listens to Winnie-the-Pooh at daddy's feet one Sunday, on Children's Hour, in the drawing room with dark pink armchairs. Pooh has a deep voice and Piglet a squeaky voice coming out of a box by the sofa. Tess wants the voices to last for ever, but also wants to pee, so sits with the right heel pressed into the peeplace, to hold the pee back. A trick discovered for when Tess doesn't want to interrupt the intensity of the moment, enjoying the fullness of the moment even with the fullness of the bladder, as against the flow of time and urine. But mummy knows the manoeuvre and lifts the child. Tess yells and floods the dark pink carpet. Winnie-the-Pee. Daddy turns away, disgusted.

A flimsy beige evening dress is lying on the big bed in the front bedroom near the front door. Tess gazes at the dress in wonder, has never seen mummy in evening dress and longs to. Mummy and daddy are going out. Annie, the Swiss au pair, is to stay on guard. Where did Annie sleep? The flat had no spare room. But Joanne is having tantrums. Like Tess with the pee, Joanne yells and screams, don't go out, don't go out. Daddy turns away, disgusted. Mummy and daddy go out.

Memory is thought of in time, but time is always represented spatially, hands round a clock, decades aligned, and today all the terms for memory are spatial, screening, filing, effacing, storing, labelling, visualizing, doors opening on doors, scope-gates on scape-goats, representing the data-structures of the world as if all philosophy and history were not Herodotage, Clio's clangers,

42

Erato's errata, rearticulation and disarticulation in the blindness of new logics.

How difficult to reimagine a state of ignorance. The old lady remembers making that effort when first learning to teach, late in life, in Paris, for at university level few teachers remember the long life of learning life. And Fatima at forty-four wanting to learn to read and write, very slow at first, BA, BA, BA for a line, then BE, BE, BE. But there is progress. By the end of the summer Fatima understands how G can be guttural before A, O, U but equal to J before E and I, unless a U is inserted: GUI, GUE, GAGA. And a triumph suddenly: JUGE. But Fatima is very busy, can't find time to do the homework, earning most of the family money, for Mohammed is unemployed, depressed and diatribal. Yet Fatima perseveres despite the husband's mockery, through the double vowels and the double consonants: grave, grève, broute, fleuve, gloire. And says neither Simone nor daughter Khadija were so patient or such fun as teachers earlier. The old lady hugs Fatima, oddly moved at this tribute to the reimagining a state of ignorance, all the way back to unrembered infancy.

The nursery at 15 Fairlawn Court Acton Lane SW15 is simply a small square room with the door on the right and two beds set at right angles on the left, each against a chest-of-drawers obliqued in the left corner. The right wall is shared with the dining-room and has a gas-fire, an orange bee-hive when lit, with an opposite number on the other side. The white bath towels dry on the brass fender smelling of scorch. At the window between the left and right walls, looking out onto other dark red blocks and small gardens, there is a table and two chairs.

Joanne draws backless evening dresses in many colours, endlessly long ladies with short shingles and long necks and arms, the shoulder bits plunging to the waist in a deep naked U-shape, the dress swelling on the hips then narrowing to immobilize the legs at the knees but flaring out flowerly below. Where does Joanne learn these things? Joanne makes Tess draw the ladies too and Tess copies obediently but badly, pretending to enjoy. Perhaps Tess's lack of clothes sense is born here. Or later, Tess always inheriting Joanne's frocks, never caring about torn or dirty clothes, wanting to be a boy as later the young scholar, pestered by men or illness, yearns to be a brain without a body. Joanne has a natural clothes-sense, whether flush or broke. Here, have this dress, out of fashion now, Joanne says when returning jobless from Kuala Lumpur or Kirkuk or Kinchassa, in the same tone used when once passing an unliked piece of cheese to grand-père, tiens, un cadeau, le fromage est mauvais.

No clothes are needed here, such relief, just slacks and sweaters or shorts and tee-shirts, and a few elegant things for London or local parties. Now the heat has at last cooled down the old lady can go off on daily walks again, up through the woods onto the plateau and down again through the vines, cutting off the many bunches of grapes left unpicked in the table-grape vine among the more acid wine-grape vines. Soon there will be the autumn gardening. Fatima will help, Fatima the delight, known to all for cleaning and charisma, illiterate and intelligent, pushing the children to study. The old lady helped daughter Khadija through the Bac English Oral, gives English lessons to Mohammed, the next in line. The Moroccans far surpass the two immediate French neighbours in human warmth.

Joanne invents the games, Joanne tells Tess to do this or that and Tess does. Joanne is the elder and better, has the talents at the piano and drawing, the imagination. This seems fair since Tess though in the same class is better at school. Joanne says all the outrageous funny things for ever repeated by grown-ups as familore. The things Tess says rarely get repeated, not being quaint or funny. Bruxelles est une ville loin seems to be Tess's only score, and only faintly quaint. But Tess takes all that as fact of life, like towns and telephones, motorcars and mountains. Another fact of life is Joanne having fair and naturally curly hair, then worn in ringlets and admired in the street by strangers. Tess has straight mousy hair, worn either ill-cut by Annie in a pudding-basin fringe or, as now, in tight little plaits never growing very long but sticking out stiffly and tightly ribboned behind the ears like low-worn horns. Joanne is pink and white, like daddy, Tess is pale and sallow, like nobody, with a face not a face at all in the glass but a splodge. Tess doesn't learn to look at that face linger-ingly till the age of nineteen, in a billet-room in Bletchley, working spare hours at Ovid's *Metamorphoses* for Higher School Cert by correspondence, at bedtime brushing hair and suddenly seeing the girl in the mirror as beautiful, examining the image in surprise and taking film-star poses. Vilain bébé jolie jeune fille?

Hey, says John[45] the focus-puller, could the old lady be dubceking memory? This meek acceptance of Joanne's betterness in all things except brains is a bit suspect.

And where is Dubcek's toe?

Envy?

There was no envy, Tess simply admired, Joanne didn't. Then, on worldly success, life slowly operated a reversal. Joanne's problems in any case aren't just towards Tess but towards all, mummy, the family, lovers and bosses and helpful friends, Joanne biting the hand of every gift-horse in the mouth.

But Tess came to stand for all, those others having failed Joanne.

Tess failed Joanne too.

But is there. To be bitten, beaten. Part of Joanne's problem, yet untrained in transfer, and so forever the wrong person to break through those pretty foggy scenarios of aparthide.

The old lady marvels at John for the things John can't do, elapse, be admired by sincerity.

Joanne and Tess playing doctors with dolls, on a Sunday morning, while daddy is listening to loud music in the drawing-room. Ghrrr, that noise, the dolls are ill, go and tell daddy to shut up, Joanne orders, go ON. Terrified, Tess takes Pooh Bear, fifth-birthday present from daddy, and creeps along the endless corridor, past the bathroom and kitchen, towards the drawing-room. The music gets louder and louder. The door is ajar. Tess pushes the door open, daddy is standing in a dark red dressing-gown by the chimney-piece with the statuette of Nefertiti. Tess daren't hesitate, throws Pooh Bear into daddy's legs shouting Shut UP and runs away screaming with daddy in angry pursuit, leaps onto the bed and clambers over the chest-of-drawers in the corner, falling into the angle-hole behind. Daddy hauls Tess out by a pigtail, smacks furiously and deprives the child of Sunday lunch. Tess cries for hours on the bed, not for daddy's anger or the loss of Sunday lunch, but at always being led, as with

Jean-Luc and the pear tree, and always punished for doing the things mentors say. Nor does mummy defend Tess. Mummy too is led. But later comforts Tess and produces a newspaper photograph. The Thames banks have burst and people are walking on chairs. Life is worse for others.

Summer holidays in La Panne, near Ostend, with Joanne, Jean-Luc and a girl called Johnny Smith, mummy and grand'mère. The sea is cold and dirty yellow, and that year full of stinging jellyfish. Tess shudders and screams, runs out shivering, to be rubbed down brutally with a rough towel. The grasses on the dunes are covered with an epidemic of black and orange caterpillars, or another year perhaps, and Tess refuses to walk, to Joanne's mockery, has to be carried yelling by grand'mère, soothing. People are dying of heat wave in London, grand'mère says, how lucky Tess is to be here by the sea.

Tess hates the sea. The sea means horrid journeys from Ostend to Dover and back on Channel-boats belching black smoke and making the horizon sink and the stomach turn and the mouth vomit carrots in yellow jellyfish. The sea has screeching seagulls swooping down on the boat, the sea has ports with cranes lifting huge boxes like houses high above heads and porters rushing up the gangway crying Porter! Porter!

The blue school is welcome. A bit further away, at Turnham Green. Learning to add horrid shillings and pence, carry twelve, carry twenty. Reading is easy now. Daddy has bought The Children's Encyclopaedia and all the Lang Fairy Books, the Red Fairy Book, the Green, the Yellow, the Violet. *The Just-So Stories*. And *The Water Babies*, read out by mummy with great enthusiasm, hated by Tess. And *Peter Pan*, hated by Tess, Tess wants to grow up. And *Uncle Remus*, read sometimes by daddy in an American twang, not understood at all by Tess. And *The Girls' Own Paper*, Betty Barton & Co, Joanne pounces on that each week, reading on the floor with Tess following more or less.

Joanne walks with Tess along the park in dark blue tunics, vyella shirts, blue ties, blue blazers and porkpie hats, the way of the English world Joanne and Tess now belong to. Getting on well, used now to new schools every year, in a different country or town or part of town. This school is bigger, with wide stairs

46

and galleries. The brown school was only a small house. There's a big road to cross and Joanne takes Tess's hand. Joanne has a great plan, changing names. Joanne and Theresa are awful, outlandish. But Tess likes Tess. Joanne's name never gets shortened. Joanne is going to be Peggy, and Tess is going to be Molly, Joanne announces at home. Mummy hits hand to head as usual, meaning either Oh-how-stupid-mummy-is-forgetting-this-or-that, or, as now, what-has-mummy-done-to-deserve-such-dreadful-children? But in the evening daddy laughs and insists for days on calling Joanne Peggy Piggins and Tess Molly Muggins. The new identities are quietly dropped. Mummy shows a picture of Princess Elizabeth and Princess Margaret Rose, nieces of King George V, ah, George, like grandpère. Princess Elizabeth is curly-haired and pretty, Princess Margaret Rose straight-haired and less pretty. Tess feels one with Princess Margaret Rose.

On Chiswick Green there is a huge tank from la grande guerre, and mummy explains how the caterpillar chains could mount over obstacles and crush everything on the way. Mummy takes the children to an afternoon pantomine in the High Street, with a china shepherd and a china shepherdess stepping down, much too large, from a chimneypiece. As usual Tess doesn't follow. Joanne and Tess are now sometimes taken on bus rides, to Ravenscourt Park or Chiswick House Grounds or Kew Gardens. Kew has a Japanese pagoda. The buses are red and have two floors, the top floor open with rubbery black covers fixed to the seats against cold and rain. The buses in front have pictures, a brown and beige picture of a small boy blowing bubbles with Coal Tar Soap, a blue and white picture of a sailor framed in a lifebelt underlined by Players Navy Cut or a gentleman in grey trousers and red jacket and top hat called Johnny Walker, walking, where to?

Christmas. The little girls wait impatiently to be allowed into the drawing-room with the tree and the presents. At last mummy opens the door and the children rush headlong towards the lit tree in the bay window, émerveillées, shrieking with joy at the new small white wooden table and chairs, where sit Pooh Bear and the dolls, and two new brown-haired dolls in blue velvet bonnets and caped coats edged in white rabbit fur, the bigger doll clearly for

Joanne, the smaller for Tess. Sylviane et Marianne, Joanne names the new dolls at once, picking up Sylviane to stroke and hug. Tess strokes Marianne. Then comes a loud disgruntling from behind. Mummy says gently: go and wish daddy a Happy Christmas. Abashed, the little girls go and hug daddy, the killjoy party nasty.

The old lady pauses, looks out, decides to go down and prepare dinner for the friends arriving in the late afternoon. August has been exhausting, with too many though welcome visits, but these friends are special, and September has given a pause. The steps are curved, narrow and perilous, to be taken slowly, like a little girl. Despite the tough walks some gestures are now difficult, standing on one foot for a second to slip on pants for instance, easier to sit on the bed, slip in both legs, then stand.

The old lady chops the summer vegetables for a daube provençale, then the lamb marinated since yesterday in wine and herbs from the garden, and places the onions, the garlic, the chopped bacon and lamb below, then the vegetables in layers according to the slowness of each, then the marinated herbs, all into the oven. Without a husband to talk to the guests, simmering dishes are easier, otherwise talk over drinks is impossible. Ah, the talk. Such a stimulating substitute for TV. All Tess's friends practise conversation as an art, rather than an aggression. Not an art of artifice, but a cultivation of natural courtesy, often unknown on French discussion programmes where all the men still talk at once, becoming unhearable, and ignorrupt the token woman.

Was party nasty responsible for a dual attitude to Christmas? For twenty-five years now the old lady has happily ignored Christmas. The most memorable is spent in Mexico, after a term's teaching in snowy Buffalo. Driving all over from pyramid to pyramid, through forests from ruin to ruin, ending at Chichen Itza on Christmas Day, at the far end of Yucatan with only two days to catch the plane in Mexico City back to Paris. There are no shops, only tourist kiosks, and the drive is done on bread and mineral water, barefoot in a summer dress, among white-capped volcanoes in the distance and along the Mexican Gulf. Heat, bread and water, solitude, Christmas inverted, reinvented. And the dual attitude to the festivity of friendship, not just now but throughout life? Genuine joy, sharing, listening, loving, then, at the end of the party, ah, alone at last. No, too easy, Tess simply took after mummy, half a hermit, without the faith. The old lady remembers the publishers' parties in the late fifties and sixties, at first the thrill at being invited at all, then quickly, the disappointment, the fatigue at the smart empty talk of the quidnappers, orbiting round the world like a dead language with an internal grammar generating only dead sentences. The singing tree wants to be a talking bird, the talking bird wants to be a thinking reed whispering how the king has ass's ears. The relief at leaving London literary life. Carefully not joining the Paris equivalent, and disliking parties with the local rich here. Mummy too was shy of people. Can happy exchange then occur only in strata, transcending ethnic and national alienations, the workers of the world uniting, the smart sets and the jet sets smarting and jetting, the rich enriching the rich, the poor impoverishing the poor, the intellectuals intellecting? The old lady has and has had many affectionate friends, but prefers intimate dinners, the wine loosening the levels, from technical to trivial, from personal to metaphysical, from highly serious to hilarious, and has always experienced this, hence the difficulty of adjusting to gatherings or to people on the single register of self. Like the family. Like Joanne. Like the two flanking neighbours here. But then, Tess also was once on a single register. How difficult to reconstruct a state of ignorance. Yet how easy to accept and love restricted minds when restriction is cancelled by open hearts, those of so many different people, truck-drivers on hitch-hikes, Waafs in barracks, wartime landladies, concierges, students, Fatima the adorable, but perhaps not enough, still can't cope when there is the barrier of self-locked scenarios, lack of human warmth and reciprocity. Christian charity does not demand reciprocity, and here the old lady, though not a Christian, has failed, does not suffer ghouls even sadly.

Party nasty on the balcony, waving good riddance.

How nasty? During the war, at Bletchley, a letter suddenly arrives, via the lawyer and via the official Air Ministry address, from daddy's sister Dorothy, complaining about a small inheritance from daddy's other sister, long in a mental home, died intestate, the sum awarded by Chancery in three parts to Dorothy,

Joanne and Tess. Tess has made over the cheque at once to mummy, and says so in reply, on Ian's priggish advice, adding some icy remark about mummy having suffered enough at the hands of Alfred Hayley. Whereupon Dorothy writes furiously: look up Marjorybank's *Life of Sir Edward Marshall Hall*, and find out all about Alfred Hayley. Exit aunt Dorothy, exit Tess's interest in Alfred Hayley, far too much work.

Years later, Tess will look up the reference. A thief, a lying mythomaniac, a cheater.

Granny and grandpère have moved to a large flat in Schaerbeek, at 55 avenue de l'Opale, near the Tir National (could grandpère be seeking the army's protection?), and the open country beyond. The quartier is new, not far from l'avenue Mahillon, and all the streets around have the names of precious stones, except rue Victor Hugo. The avenue de l'Opale is wide, with flat square cobbles and little acacia trees all along the squat houses in individual styles. Only No 55 is a five-floor block sticking out, on the corner of rue Victor Hugo.

The flat is on the fourth floor, L-shaped, with a room near the entrance for mummy and a twin-bedded double room for Joanne and Tess giving through a blue-grey door of knobbled glass onto the big parqueted entrance-hall, kitchen to the left with a balcony, a pantry and ice-basin, dining and drawing rooms to the right. All the doors and woodwork are painted blue-grey, all the radiators brown and all the walls are grey. Grand'mère and grandpère have rooms far away, along the corridor leading to the spare room and the big bathroom with two white washstands and a white tub. At the entrance to the long corridor, just before the lavatory on the left, a telephone is fixed to the wall, high at adult level, so when the children are allowed to speak the high kitchen stool has to be brought.

Joanne and Tess are sent to school dressed from top to toe in dark green kilts and jumpers and socks and tartan ties, of the Hayley tartan, bought by daddy, the Hayleys of Nairn, daddy said, and are treated as foreign bodies.

Soon after arriving at l'avenue de l'Opale for good Tess falls very ill, kidney-trouble already. Wrapped in cold wet sheets to send the soaring temperatures down, until the sheets are hot and clammy. At the highest fever Tess starts to sing in a small angelic voice and everyone goes round hushed, saying voilà la fin. Okay John, pseudo-memory, maman tells later, and nobody, least of all Tess, wonders about the link between this high infection and Tess's heel habit. Later, later, Tess will wonder. But stop looping, John, méchant loup, nasty piece of perk.

And stop evading loops, little sheep. That heel-habit, formed for the prolongation of intellectual pleasures as the old lady knows full well, must have caused the so-called congenital malformation – mais l'urèthre plonge dans le vagin! – blighting an entire sexlife, not discovered by any English gyno or uro for over thirty years, found through the simplest fingerprod in Paris and fixed, decades too late. No wonder Tess rarely enjoyed sex, feeling pain and discomfort, followed by illness. The child turned into an incongruous Sue Bridehead wanting only companionship, with sex as price to pay for love, for sharing, for affection, inspiration and guidance, an incongruous virgin of the kind pedestaled throughout European culture for innocence and sexlessness but born in a century when women are enguilted for precisely that, a century so privileging the sexual drive as to create a Deus Sex Machina, a new opium of the people, when there are so many alternative deities and drives and modes of love, now turned into abnormak repressions. And all because of an undiscovered congenital malformation. Congenital? Self-inflicted more likely.

Such an outburst! Must be John the psycho, the casting adviser, in the usual haste to blame Tess not the mysteries of creation. Down, méchant loup, stop howling. Anyway why Sue Bridehead? Why not Mrs Dalloway or Lily Briscoe and other twentieth-century virginals? The Deus Sex Machina didn't fully crank out till the sixties after all. Besides, isn't all being congenital, though men and women build on that and make do? Make do, translated once for fun as faire faire, and why not? making identities make a seamless tissue of half-lies.

Presents arrive from daddy. Joanne is wholly excluded, sleeps in the spare room. How stupid can parents get?

At Easter Tess recovers and goes with maman to Knocke-le-

Zoute. Sea-air is the universal remedy then, but bracing, not the melanogenous grilled sausages of today. The weather's bitterly cold and windy. A group of girl-guides is running up and down the steps of the sloping dyke and Tess wails envious despair at ever running like that again. Mais bien sûr, chérie. But the voice betrays doubt and fear.

Maman is right. Tess has missed many weeks at school but somehow catches up.

Somehow! Tess is caught cheating in a Flemish exam, the grammar book open on the empty seat of the two-seater desk in the last row, chosen for that purpose. But Madame Maertens, a highly made-up middle-aged lady with brown and yellow hair flattened down in careful waves, is walking towards the desk. Tess is paralysed. Madame Maertens raises the book to the whole class. Regardez, les enfants! Ooooh! Tess hands the letter to maman, hand to head slap of the how-has-maman-deserved kind, eyes thrown heavenwards. Never again. Eater seater cheater.

BUT two years later, when the same Madame Maertens summons maman to say Tess should sit for the lycée exam rather than go on into the secondary classes, maman looks at Tess doubtfully and says no, Greek and Latin, too difficult, the workload is too hard, Tess isn't strong enough.

And repeat-performance just after the war, says the nasty piece of perk, focus-puller John[45], when Tess has got into Oxford and introduces Janek. Oxford after all. And Janek seems so clever. Daddy was too clever. Will Tess be able to keep up? Yet not finding Ian too clever two years earlier when Tess tries to break that engagement. A good man is hard to find, mummy says then, as if Tess at twenty wanted a good man or any man. At least Ian will be faithful. Pushing Tess into marriage as granny did.

John please go away, go on, elapse. John, perhaps the lighting engineer after all, elapses.

The big beige Opel with the Aachen number drives into the garden. Hans and Dagmar have arrived, Dagmar much younger than Hans, Hans much younger than the old Houyhnhnm, like most friends these days. Dagmar, petite and elegant, teaches English in a school, Hans in the University, both perfectly bilingual. Hans, bearded and benign, is the last of the mentors, never like one of the toppled mentowers but kindly and constructive, a tower of strength not a tour de force. Perhaps because the old lady is long past needing mentors, has long been able to meet all mentors on undangerous flying planes of imagination, in a free exchange, no longer feeling one-upped or wanting to one-up. Growing old has exquisite compensations.

Since the last visit France has at last put unleaded petrol at all the stations and German cars need not fly-by seeking Bleifrei. How was the trip, the route taken, and travel-talk ensues and more, laughter, a stimulated listening and a scintillating transcendence of toanfroing alter ego trips et galore. But later, after hearing about the rudeness of the French on the way, the old lady tells how arriving back this Spring from lectures in the States where all are so over polite, at least in airports, and landing at Orly after a sleepless night and time lag to catch the Marseille connection, at least five people were disagreeable within half an hour and the air-hostess thoroughly unpleasant on being asked by the old lady for help in putting the medium hand-luggage on the rack: huh, should have registered that.

There seems to be something wrong with the French, says Hans with a laugh. And how are the neighbours now?

Gone.

What, all the neighbours?

No, just the two serpents. And Mme Bernard died. The whole population has changed, lovely young couple now where Suzie was.

Wait long enough and problems go away?

Well, minor problems at least. The world's don't.

And off again, on the state of the world.

5. FILE: GAMMA DELTA

The old lady is reading a delectably impatient article on child-hood-recalling books in *The London Review of Books*, imagining a new theory for the 21st century, about the crucial years of an individual's psychological development not being from birth till five, but between the ages of forty-two and forty-seven. The psyche and personality in the first half of life would be merely malleable and unfinished, childhood trauma not trauma but neutral and neural experience. People would simply be analysed between the ages of forty and forty-two and get sorted out before the critical age – the Mid-Life Crisis – and be ready to spend fruitful years from middle age to death as positive, harmonious and psycho-logically healthy Houyhnhnms.

The harmonious, healthy, hilarious Houyhnhnm neighs with delight, identification, and doubt.

Foucault denied the individual self yet surely did not become a Houyhnhnm. And yet, though not analysed at forty-two, the Houyhnhnm's second half of life was the positive harmonious healthy compensation of the late developer, while the first half was a permanently blurred intake from constantly changing mentors, and childhood a mechanically ordered dream, wiped out. Tess doesn't begin to exist until the war and even that is effaced for years by the Official Secrets Act.

For Tess is a quietly happy child in Brussels, works well, makes friends, and having or later not having a pater noster in London is neither here nor there. Or rather, Tess divides into a tomboy show-off at school and a goody-goody at home, laying the table with the blue and white plates when called. Or when not called. Grand'mère, faut mettre la table?

Non, la table est déjà là.

Bon, le couvert.

Joanne, however, goes through a stage of clambering all over maman with caresses crying paman paman paman, craving for dual affection, maman rejecting Joanne impatiently, sois tranquille.

Jeanne should never have had children, Vanna says bitterly forty years later, in Grasse. Joanne, with that pink and white look and glaring grey eyes, reminded Jeanne daily of Alfred.

Translate: And Tess didn't, being totally Blair (or Vanderbilt). Unfair to Joanne. The middle-aged Tess tries to explain repetition compulsion, the repetition for ever of that double rejection, Joanne behaving in such a way as to force people into rejection. Tante Vanna is dubious about such facile explanations

But grand'mère had a good relationship with Joanne, Jeanne always said, grand'mère consoled Joanne, understood Joanne. Remembering, perhaps, not being perfect once.

Yes, Joanne loved grand'mère. But grand'mère died.

There is a religious procession coming up l'avenue de l'Opale and Tess cries out at the bishop's yellow canopy in the distance, regarde, le marchand de glaces! Family laughter. Complètement stupide, says Joanne delightedly, l'évêque un marchand de glaces! Tess laughs obligingly.

Joanne also collects glossy black postcards of glamorous film stars and imposes the mania on Tess in a strangely faked rivalry, maman having to buy one each at a time, Jean Harlow, Loretta Young, Anna May Wong, Lilian Harvey, Annabella, Greta Garbo, Joan Bennett, and others. Where does Joanne get this kind of knowledge from? Grandpère spoke fondly of Greta Garbo yesterday, but also of someone called Joséphine Baquère and someone else called Rabelais. Tess stares at the unknown faces, meaningless to children rarely taken to the cinema, and then only to Charlie Chaplin, Harold Lloyd balancing on skyscrapers, Maurice Chevalier singing *Louise* to Jeannette Macdonald on a leafy terrace, *A Midsummernight's Dream, Little Women* with Katherine Hepburn and *Captains Courageous* with Freddie Bartholomew, the last image a wreath on the water, Tess having no idea of the drowned character, and dark Bartholomew most unconvincing as little Lord Fauntleroy, blond and sissy, read as book but with distaste. Except for *Little Women*, loved as book, Tess doesn't follow the films at all. The old lady has ever since marvelled at the way everyone at the time, however uneducated, so quickly grasped the language of the cinema, with the quick cuts in mid-conversation and the flash-backs pluperfected in music or fades. Tess is a book-world child.

On Saturdays Oncle Francis, Tante Mathilde and Jean-Luc come. Oncle Francis is dark and sleek, Tante Mathilde slim with brown and yellow hair, juste passés à la camomille, and flatters grandpère with much attention and laughter. Tante Mathilde is always sidérée by everything. Jean-Luc's fair hair has turned brown, and less curly, no longer Fauntelroyal. Grand'mère makes the same meal, boiled chicken and rice with a piquant yellow sauce. Or, in warmer weather, cold chicken and salad with a mayonnaise Tess learns to make, stirring hard with one hand, holding the oil bottle with the other for only a drop at a time to fall in. Sometimes grand'mère makes orange jelly, turning the tall kitchen stool upside down, placing a large bowl inside, tying a white cloth to the legs and pouring the hot dark mixture into the cloth for Tess to stir until all the juice has filtered through into the bowl, poured then into a fish-shaped dish placed in the ice-basin.

And grand'mère takes the children down town to the toy-department of the Galleries Anspach. Town is always down, descendre en ville, though Belgium is flat, the yellow trams seem to gravitate swiftly into the pear-shaped centre learnt at school, towards the Voyages Blair between Sainte Gudule and the Grand'Place, all golden and visited in school excursions. Like the Cinquantenaire, the Palais Royal, huge and hideous, the Parc Royal with the round pond and jet d'eau, and minuscule rarely visible bits of a river called La Senne, a very poor relation of La Seine. Maman never goes to town with the children, only on walks, dressed in a long brown tweed coat with beige lamb collar and brown hat, and seems very absent except for a wake-up kiss and early breakfast before school at eight, and a goodnight kiss. But teaches Tess English songs, *The raggle-taggle gypsies* and *Oh, no John no John no John no*, both songs of lady's refusal Tess loves. And makes pretty dresses, exactly alike, for Joanne and Tess,

Tess inheriting Joanne's and therefore wearing each for longer, though spoiling each more quickly. And there are joint family expeditions, all three families, to Tervueren, to Quatre Bras, to Laeken.

Joanne and Tess share the twin-bedded room at first, and when Jean-Luc comes Joanne is lent maman's room next door. Jean-Luc and Tess can hear Joanne jumping up and down in admiration at the drawings of fashions or follies or funny faces done all afternoon. After grand'mère's death Joanne is given mummy's room and Tess has the double-room, with only one bed, in the corner, facing the large window with the false balcony. But Joanne's piano stays, and Joanne comes in every day to play, amazingly, able to reproduce tunes by ear and harmonize and sight-read notes like words. Tess is much more elementary, but one day plays *La Matchiche*, a piece learnt from a popular book, and grandpère comes storming from the other end of the flat and forbids Tess to play that. So Tess plays *La Matchiche* occasionally to bring on the storm. On the wall above the bed mummy's photograph follows Tess all round the room with dark eyes, tender, reproachful, astonished, pleased. That photograph, mummy in short wavy dark hair, often feels closer than the original.

Jean-Luc invents a new game called Nanouk, after a film about an Eskimo prisoner pulling at manacles. A deck-coit is placed at the centre of the twin-beds and tugged, each from one side, until the other is drawn across.

Can't have been Nanouk, says John the pedant. O'Flaherty's *Nanouk of the North* was made in 1922, a pure documentary, no Eskimo pulling at manacles, only pulling at a seal below the ice and being drawn on the stomach almost into the hole with the effort.

Perhaps Jean-Luc was thinking of that.

Why not ring Jean-Luc?

And Jean-Luc laughs, remembers the scene with manacles vividly, adding blood pouring down the wrists for good memory-measure, suggests some other film, an adventure film, was made later, using the name Nanouk. But can't remember, can't hunt, nor is the old lady going to travel to the cinémathèque in Paris to find out.

And trains, dinky cars, meccano, brought for the purpose, or a chemical set, or a film-projector with Félix le Chat. Jean-Luc has many toys. And football down the long corridor, Tess standing just below the high telephone, the goals being the big hall at one end and the spare room at the other. All boys' games, Tess as usual aquaescing, happily losing identity to mentors. In Spring there is also playing in the street, almost empty of cars, except for an occasional milk-cart drawn by a poor St Bernard dog. Or cycling behind the Tir National, or taking two yellow trams to Tervueren alone, heads hanging out among the trees of the Forêt de Soignes. And seeing all those places again forty-five years later on a drive with Jean-Luc, all so different, the Tir National now the huge glass and steel radio station. The school on Boulevard Clovis, now ironically a lycée, still black and like a prison, with the black brick playyard where the lavatories were. And incredibly small.

Jean-Luc also invents a mountaineering game, played in the drawing-room after the grown-ups have left for rest or work, and consisting of having to climb on the furniture never touching ground. The modern furniture is in fact set round the walls, leaving a large empty centre of parquet. The arrangement, come to think, betrays a peculiar social life. First a grey velvet reclining chair in the left corner, then the antique chest of drawers with the old wooden panière on top, like a chapel, of moulded wooden bars (so how were the mice kept out?), now housing the wireless loudspeaker. A grey velvet tub-chair with little round brass tacks all round the back, then a dangerous leap onto the bottom shelf of a marble-topped fern-plant bearer in the bay window, more grey tub-chairs round the forbidden territory of a carved brasstop coffee-table, onto grandpère's grey reclining armchair, then the sofa, easy, covered with shawls, followed by the perilous tall stand with the wind-up gramophone on top, and then, triumphantly, the last tub-chair by the wide opening to the dining-room. The gramophone could play a song called *Cheek to cheek*, sung in daddy's voice, and a lady playing a cello to a nightingale, as well as Bach fugues Tess would dance to, imitating Alexandre and Clotilde Sakharov, seen at the Beaux Arts.

In quieter moods, Tess and Jean-Luc invent a story also enacted the adventures of Grand Frère et Petite Soeur, though Tess is a year older, and write the story down in an exercise book, or rather, Tess writes, Jean-Luc dictates, Joanne later illustrating, a huge temple in the Brazilian jungle, a little black girl, a treasure.

The exercise-book, remember, says Tess on meeting Jean-Luc again in Brussels at 56 and 55, Les Aventures de Grand Frère et Petite Soeur? Tess found the book in a trunk recently, exactly the same, with Joanne's drawings. Jean-Luc is eager to see. But back in Paris, about to leave for Jerusalem to teach, Tess hunts in every drawer, every file, in vain. Tess has no trunk. Perhaps the book was in the Brussels trunk, with the toys, or in the Old Kent Road trunk, with Pooh Bear, both reopened after the war, Tess can't remember, can't imagine finding yet not retrieving the book. The discovery was merely a recent dream, but with all the reality of absolute conviction, perhaps in anticipation of meeting Jean-Luc again after over forty years.

Joanne and Tess walk to school together at first, along the small acacias and the flat cobbled pavements and irregular houses, towards the Place Jambline de Meux with the triangle of laburnums, on to the Place des Gueux where the yellow trams stop and turn, down the dreary Rue des dreary Confédérés to the Boulevard Clovis. One early morning in the Place Jambline de Meux, just about where the music teacher lives, a man is pushed out of a door, trousers wide open at eye-level. At school Joanne tells, others tell, and Madame Maertens takes Tess and Joanne apart for a scolding. But Tess has no clear idea of the sight seen, if at all, only an astonishment at the fuss.

Le roi Albert dies in a climbing accident in the Ardennes and the class is made to collect newspaper photographs into albums, the young King Leopold walking behind the coffin, and beautiful Queen Astrid, a bit like maman but with flat hair, and the three children, la princesse Joséphine-Charlotte, le prince Baudouin, le prince Albert. But Tess feels the distance this time, with three not two, and only one girl, the eldest, and two boys.

Later, Joanne and Tess walk separately, with separate friends. The class has been split in two, though of the same level, and Joanne has been placed in the other, perhaps wisely to avoid envy at Tess's better marks. Joanne's friend is Nadine, very sophisticated, a bad influence mummy says. Tess's friend is Liliane, and when the bell rings Tess leaps down the stairs two by two for five floors noisily rather than take the lift, as Joanne does. Liliane persuades Tess to join a Catholic club for children, to maman's delight, meaning chiefly meeting in some small hall and playing musical chairs after saying the Je vous salue Marie to a statue of a woman in blue and white. No explanations about the woman or the fruit of entrails or Sainte Marie merde Dieu, repeated by rote, the organizing ladies taking Tess's catechismic knowledge for granted.

Tess likes looking out of the fifth-floor window onto the lower roofscape, sometimes seeing grand'mère, heavily laden, struggling up the rue Victor Hugo from the market near l'avenue Mahillon, behind la caserne, still preferred to local shops. Grand'mère seems to do most of the work. Apart from early breakfast before school, maman is always tired, resting on the bed.

One day maman suddenly talks about going to live in Paraguay.

Paraguay! Where's Paraguay?

Amérique du Sud, imbécile, says Joanne.

Well, Paraguay's much cheaper. The money daddy sends would go further.

Tess has never thought about daddy sending money, nor about money going anywhere, near or further. Where does maman get these sudden ideas? Maybe from Oncle Francis and the Voyages Blair.

The family is not rich, yet Tess has no feeling of being poor. But grandpère keeps talking of la crise, and receives a glossy illustrated magazine called L'URSS in huge red letters. Everything is better in L'URSS. Every evening grandpère listens to news from L'URSS on the TSF, and nobody's allowed in the drawing-room. La Grande Ourse, perhaps, grandpère taught Tess to recognize la Grande Ourse from the window. Apparently up there in the black sky there is no crise.

Yet there are holidays. Oh, modest. Easter at Knokke in a small pension, where Tess gets otitis and sees Joanne mouthing with furious gestures like a silent film. And summers in Switzerland, on a farm in Lovatens, Canton de Vaud. Tante Dora is also there with Daniel and three tiny blonde sisters. Tess seems to have an instinct for grabbing the only male around to play with. Joanne has to follow catch-up classes at the village school while Daniel and Tess swing on the parallel bars outside or jump endlessly in a barn from one level of hay to another. But all walk together through the forest to Bulle, in the canton de Fribourg, where the cows are black and white, like the Fribourg flag and Tess asks why the cows in Vaud aren't green and white. One day maman takes Tess and Joanne down a steep wide path through woods to Lucens, in the valley, to have tea with an old lady, warning over and over against expectations as the old lady's poor. The tea is lavish, with cakes and strawberries and cream, and Joanne exclaims, mais maman, la dame n'est pas si pauvre! Joanne's gaffes are still loving lore at the time, but at forty or fifty become less charming to the family and get repeated with more exasperated spite. But Vanna for years tells as funny the story of how Joanne at seven, after a brief stay at the in-law's house in Paris with maman and Tess, is given flowers for Madame Babelon mère and says: Pour le logement.

After the second summer in Lovatens grand'mère comes and takes Joanne and Tess to Geneva, to stay with Oncle Walter and Tante Laurette and Josette, a tall girl, and Eric, a little boy with a large mouth, in Grange Canal, a big house with a garden full of trees. Eric is walking on stilts and tries to teach Tess, while Joanne talks grandly upstairs with Josette. That night Tess wakes up yelling. Grand'mère and tante Laurette come in, why etc. and Tess sobs out: Si maman mourrait!...Mais chérie etc. In fact, back in Brussels, la ville loin, maman is in hospital and the children are taken to visit. But the bed is empty and made-up and Tess yells again. But maman is on the balcony, on a deck-chair, and later goes away to Sainte Maxime.

There is also the summer in Carqueiranne, near Toulon, a few years later. The three children are put on the PLM night-train wagon-lit and travel alone, can't open the loo and use the shiny metal spittoon fixed to the floor. Tess wakes to hear Vienne, Valence, and wonders why the train is going through Austria and Spain. Jean-Luc already went last year and plays knowing. The holiday-home for children is an old martello-tower on a promontory, the dining-tables are in the moat. There is a siesta under the pines on the way down to the beach listening to *Vingt mille lieues sous les mers*, with Tess falling asleep. The sea is warm and buoyant, Tess and Joanne learn to swim. On the other side of the large bay the Hyères peninsula sticks out in the distance, or maybe islands, and Jean-Luc says look, Africa, and Tess gazes at Africa. Jean-Luc usually goes on different holidays, to more exotic places. In September the three children are collected by Oncle Francis and Tante Mathilde and drive back through France, brown as petits nègres. The dark limbs against the white bathtub in Brussels bucks Tess for weeks. The Martello tower, seen many years later with Janek, is a German bunker used as lavatory, and today has become a smart villa on the promontory, with a *vue imprenable*, since no one can build on the sea or on vertical rock.

Since Carqueiranne, Tess has hardly seen Joanne. Not only separate classes but separate holidays, camping in the Ardennes with the YWCA but Joanne refuses to go and is sent to friends in Chardonne, above Vevey. Joanne was born in Chardonne, in the Pension Bellevue run by these friends. One day Tess spots Joanne from the high window, crossing the street on a late way back from school. A shock. Joanne is wearing a grey suit, with a long skirt to the shins, looks tall and slim, comme maman, clearly made by maman without Tess noticing, looks like someone else, a grown-up, a lady. Tess is still in short skirts, and grubby.

The life of the grown-ups in Brussels is a routine, and very unlike the Stylish Drama of the Thirties seen on BBC World. Grandpère works part-time at the Voyages Blair, but comes back late, around seven, from playing billiards, at least Tess supposes so, can't imagine grandpère dancing *La Matchiche* at over seventy. Or else, the old Houyhnhnm wonders, why not? But grandpère is white-haired, solid and senatorial. There are few friends, and always the same, les Francis, Francis's partner, sometimes a director from Liège or Mons. Once a Russian lady for tea. Once a visit from Tante Alice, speaking nasal American. Or the Well-Meaning Aunts, Vanna, Dora, Laurette and husband Walter. The only grand reception is on New Year's Eve, after Tess and Joanne have gone to bed, peeping at the arrivals. The same crowd, but also the Swiss Minister, as the ambassador is called.

Daddy comes over twice, irritating the family with criticisms and complaints about everything being better in England, just like Joanne later about England versus Wherever, Hong Kong, Cairo, Syria, Tangiers. Daddy wants tram windows open if shut or vice versa. Tess is horrified, sees daddy as old, more like grandpère but flabbier, less dignified. Grandpère would never have hauled Tess out of a hiding-place by a pigtail. And once daddy's sister comes, aunt Dorothy, a replica, a fussy fair-haired elderly lady all pink and white like Joanne, charming grandpère but exasperating maman into contained fury, talking of very dear friends in South Africa, Banbury, Newmarket, always receiving so well. A sponger, says maman, and aunt Dorothy does seem to stay a long time.

A long time. For all these fragments tumbling pêle-mêle seem like forgotten photographs out of a drawer, each leading to another, static anecdotes with no narrative power, except perhaps to John le méchant loop, no montage (where is the cutting assistant?), having little to do with the middle-aged woman at mummy's death, the wife of Janek, the young WAAF officer of the war, the old lady of today, a Greerly grey-invisible. Shown alien family photographs the old lady would just as easily claim these as real past, like the girl in *Blade Runner*.

Yesterday the Prime Minister (image) attacked the position of the Eurosceptics (image of one Eurorebel in Parliament Square on background of moving traffic) in planning to vote for the Opposition's amendment (image of Labour leader at desk and papers) in favour of the Social Chapter (image of document called Social Chapter), merely to bring down the government. But the Government will not be defeated (green and brown image of empty House of Commons, synthetic image of House of Commons in statistical blue and red and yellow and pink).

The vineyards stretching towards the wooded hills of evergreen oak and pines, have turned red and orange, the cherry-orchards dark crimson against the yellowing poplars, golden in the setting sun. Soon the cherry tree leaves will vanish, leaving the branches grey. Now is the time when fires are allowed again, and all the summer's weeds and cut branches of roses and holly-hocks, piled up behind the garage, must be burnt, over many days.

The Government is defeated but tables a motion of confidence and wins, the Eurorebels brought to heel but proud (image of Eurorebel in Parliament Square etc). Strange how the prefix Euro, so enthusiastically tagged for years to every concept and product, Eurovision, Eurotransport, Eurocom, Eurofrites, Eurostek, has suddenly become Euroyahoo.

The image has no duration. And yet the image persists, returns in different guises, can serve different contexts, even without a text or rubric, existing as reality for a moment and vanishing, out of time and into memory. Images in the mind must necessarily be images of the past, already lived, already filmed, called up by clicking some kind of key.

The only memory still firm, personal and alive, is of grand'-mère's death, in 1933, while asleep. Tess is greeted with the news on returning alone from school, ringing with a special code, and is hushed by maman as the door opens. The hush is prolonged for days. The family arrives from all over. Tess is terrorized on the way to the bathroom, walking along the corridor past grand'-mère's room. The door, closed before, is open. Grand'mère lies there under an eiderdown of flowers, smelling of faint rot. Sud-denly the eyes open, then close at once on seeing Tess. Tess runs screaming back. The next day there's a brief service in the drawing-room and Tess and Joanne watch the funeral procession from the window. Joanne seems unaffected by grand'mère's death. At supper, grandpère asks Tess the colour of grand'mère's eyes. Blue. Because grandpère's eyes are blue. Comment! Forgotten so soon? And Tess weeps into the bouillon, the tears joining the small golden rings of richness and the innumerable little letters made of pasta.

The following year, same scenario with the bell, zing, zing, zing-zing-zing, maman greets Tess with the same hush, telegram in hand. Daddy est mort. Tess and Joanne miss afternoon school, for Oncle Francis and Tante Mathilde arrive with Jean-Luc, and after lunch take maman and the three kids piled into the small car to the airfield at Evere, beyond the Tir National, into a large hut, and maman walks across the grass and climbs into a fragile-looking aeroplane, a biplane says Jean-Luc, and knows the make and number. Regarde, les hélices tournent. The biplane trundles off, lifts shakily, flies away to daddy's death. But the effect is almost nil. Daddy's been dead for ages.

And then? says John[21]. John[21], the script-writer, is young and likes and-then narrative.

Facts are meaningless, John, unless reconstructed by experience.

Reconned.

Mere episodes are like soap, chunks can be missed and nothing much has moved. Or remakes of old records, putting in the cracks for verisimilitude.

Isn't life a story?

No. A story is arranged. Life is a file. A lot of files, mostly erased, the diskette to be copied erasing the diskette receiving the copy.

Don't copy then, invent, says John le méchant loop.

And time. Diskettes wear out, like the brain.

The old Houyhnhnm has just been frightened by opening a review of literary theory, put by for later reading, and discovering all the articles saliented through in pink.

All those thoughts, those arguments, those proofs, a lost turgidversation. Having climbed on books spine by spine, the old Houyhnhnm has kicked the ladder away, the ladder made of a million trillion molecules, muscles, veins. But unlike the philosopher the old lady cannot simply sit at the top like a narrative sentence and say the whole truth of being lies here. All those images resurging, merging, coupled and procreating, flowing from the brain to the fingers to the pen or keyboard, for what, to recapture some sort of egoid before going gaga?

Better hurry then.

Provence is not Providence, John.

Silence at the id-game.

6. FILE: EPSILON

And then one September, well, 1936, at thirteen, Tess returns from camping in the Ardennes and Joanne returns from the friends in Chardonne above Vevey to learn the news. No more school at the Boulevard Clovis, no more Brussels with grandpère. Oncle Francis and Tante Mathilde are coming to the avenue de l'Opale to look after grandpère. Joanne and Tess are going to a boarding school in England. Like Betty Barton & Co, remember? Vaguely.

There should have been an inkling, with Paraguay, but Paraguay came and went.

Joanne is calm but Tess wails and clamours, inverting the usual roles. What about Liliane? Oh, la grosse Liliane, Joanne scorns. And Régine, the new camping friend? Régine's mother Madame Jakob calls all children petite crotte, to Tess's delight. Une sale petite juive, says Joanne, and Tess doesn't understand.

Tess doesn't understand anything, though maman explains, Joanne and Tess being English must finish school in England. Daddy left no money, and maman will have to get a job, can't go on living at grandpère's expense. But the school is very nice, in Folkestone, or rather, just above Hythe, with big gardens, and playing-fields, and a view of the sea from all the classrooms and dormitories.

Tess hates the sea, except at Carqueiranne.

And above all, the school is for young ladies, no picking up of a horrible accent.

What's a horrible accent? Like l'accent belge?

But Tess and Joanne haven't picked up bruxellois at school here, except in fun, and talk like the family. Besides, the mistresses and the other directors of the Voyages Blair have Belgian accents, even the king, et alors?

Twenty years later, says John the loop, accents at last don't matter any more, even in England.

Ow, rarely? drawls young John, still upwardly mobile.

And the accent the girls do pick up is a horrible posh accent, says the loop. And that's never more than the temporarily winning dialect.

Joanne, however, gets the point at once.

Another train, another horrid boat, and the familiar arrival between identical little black brick houses and back-gardens as the boat-train slows down towards Victoria. A big black square cab, then the unfamiliar arrival into the large courtyard of the black brick buildings called Holbein House. Here maman has been lent a first-floor but very dark flat by a friend, with a small drawing-room of sinky armchairs and a cradled black telephone as in films, and two bedrooms. But lace curtains, and grimy, everything in London is grimy, collars and underwear are grimy in a day, the building is grimy. Tess and Joanne are miserable.

On the big double bed maman cuddles and comforts Tess, a rare occurrence, saying petite fille aux sourcils bien dessinés. That's the first and last time maman pays Tess a compliment, and the first time Tess hears something good about that splodge of a face.

The girls are taken to Daniel Neale, to be fitted with uniforms, bottle-green this time, like those kilts but less dark. Green tunics, green red and white ties, green porkpie hats and coats and blazers, vyella shirts, beige lisle stockings, green woolly knickers, white woolly vests, brown shoes, paler grey-green grosgrain dresses to change into after games and, surprise, red and white striped cotton dresses for summer. The school's colours are dark green white and dark red.

Notions of the new poverty and all these expensive purchases clash in Tess's head. Where's the money coming from? With grand'mère's lessons in economy somewhere behind the anguish. Grandpère has sold some last shares (what are shares? shares of what?), and the school is taking the girls for nothing or next to nothing, a next grandpère will presumably also pay for. But how? Why?

Remember Johnny Smith, at La Panne?

Yes (real name Diana, built a much smarter sandcastle than Tess's mess, a model castle and won mummy's prize).

Well, Johnny went to this school. Johnny's becoming a model.

A model?

Un mannequin, silly, says Joanne.

Johnny's parents, Pat and Alan Smith, were good friends of daddy's in Chiswick. Mr Smith is very rich. (So the beige evening dress was for that.) Pat approached the school and the nuns have agreed to take hardly any fees.

The nuns! Joanne exclaims and Tess silently echoes. A convent?

Not exactly. The school is run by an Anglican Order (What's Anglican? What's an Order?) but the teachers are lay (what's lay?). The Smiths have been very kind. This flat belongs to Pat's mother, a charming old lady.

Joanne and Tess are in a fusion of confusion, resentment and apprehensive wonder, and strangely unite against all this upheaval. Joanne is pleased, at any rate, with the address of Holbein House, Sloane Square, though well behind Sloane Square, almost in Pimlico. A good address is very important, Joanne says.

What's good about the address? Tess can't see the sky, and all the houses are black.

South West, stupid, absolutely essential not to have an East in the address, the East End, the slums. And SW3 is much better than SW15 in Chiswick. And Sloane Square's very smart.

How does Joanne know these things?

So the trunks are packed and sent, and off again on the train, from Charing Cross this time, and not the boat-train. There are other girls in green, in charge of a tall auburn Miss Clark, all new girls and shy, the others went yesterday. At Folkestone, taxis to St Simeon's College, SSC, on a hill above Hythe, and the new girls tumble out to be greeted on the porch of a huge house of dark red brick and ivy, by a huge benevolent nun in black and white. The fat nun kisses each girl. A shock: the chin and cheeks are prickly, like those of grandpère. This soon becomes a cruel joke, does Jam have to shave once a day or twice? Sister Jean-Marian, or Jam. The dormitories. Joanne and Tess are together, in opposite beds by the door, with six others, the head and subhead of the dorm having the beds by the big bow-window. Tess gazes at the hateful sea, guessing at hazy France, and feels homesick for a country almost unknown, exactly as Joanne once boasted France is bigger than England.

Joanne and Tess are in fact treated as French, since nobody seems to know where Belgium is. A great curiosity in such an English school at the time. Teased, questioned, giggled at. Just like the kilts in Brussels. Suddenly closer than before again, talking about the others with a Brussels accent so as not to be understood. As usual the closeness doesn't last and drifts over the terms into separate friends, separate dormitories.

But children need routine and fall in fast: filing along a glacial glassed corridor into the gym for morning prayers, greeted by a martial march, behind the head of the form and in order of the week's marks, read out every Saturday, the teachers standing against the palisades to the right. Singing a hymn and a psalm and saying the Creed, then filing out to another martial march. Lessons at nine, then gathering in the gym again to walk round arm in arm in twos or fives or tens, queuing to the bell in form-order and filing out along the glassed corridor strewn with prefects saying stop talking, into the dining-room round separate tables headed by a teacher or prefect, Jam saying grace for stews potatoes soggy cabbage and puddings. Lacrosse on the playing fields, sticks bashing on chilblains, a game never heard of since, then tea with more stodge, then prep under supervision, then the whole gym-corridor farce again for supper, then bed. A very different routine from Brussels, where school, half an hour away, started at eight, with a two-hour break at twelve to walk home for lunch, back at two, till four, then home for homework without supervision, the only ceremonial a filing past the directrice with a bow of the head in the big hall. No prefects, no sport except an hour's volley-ball in the gym once a week.

Tess wonders how anything can be learnt with so few lesson-hours, three a day instead of six, no gathering of newspaper photos for albums about the death of le roi Albert then la reine Astrid, no historical excursions to the equivalent of old Brussels, Waterloo, Anvers, Bruges, Namur, Dinant, only the clomping crocodile walks along the Lees. History is now Whigs and Tories,

Fox, Pitt, The Great Reform Bill, Canning, Peele, Clive of India, the Black Hole of Calcutta, the Indian Mutiny, the Crimean War, the Sick Man of Europe, the Corn Laws, Irish Home Rule, Disraeli, Gladstone, the Boer War. Belgium has disappeared.

Only one of the teachers is a nun, Sister Helen Muriel, the deputy head, called Ghost because floating around silently. Ghost was the first person seen, with questions, and once again Tess and Joanne are placed in the same form, first the Fourth as Juniors, later the Fifth and Sixth as Seniors, in another house near the tennis courts. The other nuns are visible in Chapel only. On Saturdays the Juniors sit on the floor of the large Common Room, mending stockings and knicker elastics under supervision, with gramophones blaring from different groups, *A Tisket, a Tasket, A brown and yellow basket, The Umberella Man*, and such. The Seniors are allowed to dance together to all those tunes, *Love Walked In, Change Partners*, foxtrots and slowsteps and tangos in the Senior Common Room. The auburn-haired Miss Clark teaches English to the Juniors, *Julius Caesar*, Walter de la Mare, W.H. Davies, and Ghost to the Seniors, *Macbeth, Hamlet*, Bacon's *Essays, Ode to the West Wind, Isabella and the Pot of Basil, The Ancient Mariner, Christabel, Paradise Lost Book I*. Miss Latouche, the plain thin drawing-mistress with a fringe, soon raves about Joanne's talent, but in the second year does not return, and the girls rumour around, Miss Latouche committed suicide out of disappointed love. Tess is shocked, not only on Joanne's behalf but at the notion of teachers having private lives and troubles. Joanne is also raved about by the music teacher Miss Swaffield, and soon plays the marches and hymns at prayers on Saturdays, to Tess's proud delight. Miss Stevens, the maths and science mistress, does take the Senior class out on botany walks to identify a nelm, a noak, a nash, and weeds called Jack-by-the-Hedge and Johnny-go-to-Bed-at-Noon. And beautiful algebra.

There follows, inevitably, baptism, and religious instruction from Jam. Tess's notions of God are derived from books like *Little Women*, as a word used in sad times, a vague entity appealed to, often in vain. Tess has never heard of Jesus Christ. The Je vous salue Marie to a plaster statue meant nothing except maman was

70

pleased, probably leaning already, or converted, but explaining nothing. Not even the Facts of Life. The tummy, yes, shyly, during a walk in the Parc Josaphat, but not how the baby gets there. Victorian prudery, the old lady now reflects, over by the nineties in some circles, nevertheless got transmitted from mother to daughter way beyond the roaring twenties in others. News today moves so fast, ideas still so slowly. Much of what the feminists are saying today, in a more complicated and historically conscious way, had been said by 1923, the year of Tess's birth, either too artistically or too inartistically. Ideas get laughed, despised and stifled out of sight but return like history. Someone in the thirties had written about future shortage of oil and other planetary resources, someone in the fifties about chemical pollution of land and sea, someone else about the waste society.

Still, Tess fits in as usual, so much easier to aquaesce, and even enjoys Scripture classes, with the slides, through a haze about the point of religion, apart from not bullying and keeping a word of honour and having good deportment and giving up pocket-money for the Order's charity-work on the Isle of Dogs (*dogs?*). Told over and over, this is not the Catholic Church of Rome, though the daily Creed says the Holy Catholic Church. No pope, no Virgin Mary. Nor does mummy participate or come down to Confirmation, in green uniform with a white head-cloth, by the Bishop of Dover. Content to let things be, better Anglican than nothing at all, to repair, perhaps, the earlier nothing at all.

Stranger still is the convention of crackpots, or crushes. The pressure to have a crackpot gets at Tess, merging as usual and choosing a rather plain girl with glasses, head of the school. The convention involves only little notes and sweets and giggling while passing at prayers. There were no crackpots in Brussels, just real friends. Later, juniors get cracked on Tess. Joanne of course despises the whole thing.

Tess stops reading altogether, except for class work, having lost the desire to read in French, grown out of the children's books – the Comtesse de Ségur chiefly, or *Sans famille* or *Le Capitaine Fracasse*, and no French books are available anyway. Unable yet to read the books the other girls read, *Lorna Doone, The Tower of London, A Tale of Two Cities, Wuthering Heights,*

The Thirty-Nine Steps, all far too dense. Tess is in a bilingual block, once reading out 'misled' as mizzled, astonished at the laughter.

Every Sunday after tea the Senior girls have to gather round Jam in flowing black robes and mend stockings, listening to thrilling instalments from *Victoria Four-Thirty* by the best-selling Cecil Roberts, as Tess daydreams, unable to follow. One Sunday Jam says there is a pamphlet called *Moral Rearmament* at the girls' disposal, inviting each to come and take a copy. Dutifully Tess does so, and can't understand a word. The following Sunday Jam complains, only one girl came, and turns to Tess: was the pamphlet interesting, Tess? Yes, Sister, mumbled in a furious blush.

Tess bluffs out as always, reversing the old split between goody-goody at home and tomboy show-off at school into goody-goody in class and tomboy show-off in recreation. Such a show-off, Tess, says Janet Weston, a prefect. So Tess becomes goody-goody all round. Bleeding one day and queuing at Matron's, frightened, but Matron merely hands out some sanitary towels and belt and pins, explaining the use but nothing else. Joanne seems to know and talks about the curse, the only advantage of the curse being the excuse from games and gym. Why do Joanne and the other girls seem to know things Tess doesn't? These things are facts of life, like Joanne's startling looks and superiority in all things except school work and games. In fact Tess learns to like both gym and lacrosse, but Joanne scorns these vulgarities, and Tess is perpetually torn between following instinct or mentors of the moment. But Tess does follow Joanne in despising the yearned for badges and colours won in sport, just like girl guides and boy scouts, says Joanne, might as well be in the army.

Tess goes through school unaware of the world, for Current Affairs are not taught, the wireless not heard. Just hearing things vaguely. There's a war in Spain. There's been a war in Abyssinia, the Negus spoke at the League of Nations. There's a fire at the Crystal Palace, wherever that is. The king abdicates, like Charlequint, much to the other girls' excitement while Tess hasn't ever heard of a deevorsee. There's a coronation, with little lights and big flags everywhere. Jean Harlow dies, Tess vaguely remembers Jean Harlow from the collected postcards. The

Zeppelin explodes somewhere, mistily recalling La Grande Guerre and those metallic caterpillar tanks. There's a war in China. Tess is frightened by the sight of screeching bombs falling from aeroplanes in occasional newsreels during the holidays.

The holidays. The holidays are much more painful. Mummy has a job as a secretary at £2.10.0 a week with the Electrical Women's Association, whatever that is. The borrowed flat has been given up for a smaller, darker, unfurnished ground-floor flat in Holbein House, at seventeen shillings and elevenpence a week, with three tiny square rooms: a sitting-room, with an anthracite stove, no central heating of course as there was in Brussels and is at school, the middle bedroom, the end one for Joanne and Tess, and no bathroom, the washing is done freezing at the kitchen sink, the loo just beyond. The furniture is from Brussels, heavy and cluttering. Later this flat too is given up for a two-room ground-floor flat at fifteen and eleven a week, the sitting-room doubling as mummy's bedroom.

Every day mummy leaves early for work, and every day the girls, never taught to cook, walk to the office for lunch à trois, through Pimlico to Buckingham Palace, huge and creamy, enjoying the sudden airy space round the white wedding-cake statue of Queen Victoria, then along the tree-lined Mall, up the Duke of York's steps, past the German Embassy where a fluffy red chow sits panting a blue tongue. Ribbentrop's dog, Joanne says, as if Tess understood. Then up Lower Regent Street, collecting mummy at the office and eating for one-and-sixpence each at Lyon's Teashop, between Piccadilly and Leicester Square, where a huge ad of Johnny Walker faces the Haymarket, legs swinging back and forth, still walking. The red buses are rarely open-decked now, most of the tops have been covered with red roofs curved at the edges and looking like slow moving houses.

One evening mummy tells about once being so hungry on the way back, just before payday with only a penny left, and going into Victoria Station to get a bar of chocolate from a machine, but getting a platform ticket. Mummy laughs. But Tess becomes suddenly aware of the hole four and sixpence a day for lunch must make in mummy's budget. And of Joanne being cruelly tiresome, demanding holiday clothes, called mufti, more outings

73

to talk about at school, complaining incessantly about the impossibility of inviting school-friends to this slum, and mummy never comes down for Saturday outings like other parents at least once a term.

Mummy tries to explain, patiently, there is no money, daddy left nothing, only some valueless shares in the company, died in debt, the Trustees, what does that mean, once forking out a small sum but that's gone. And daddy left the furniture and private belongings to that woman, mummy adds bitterly. But Joanne seems not to hear, or to listen, doesn't notice how hard mummy works, getting up early and coming back late to cook, while Joanne and Tess do nothing all day except quarrel or read the William books or Agatha Christies from the penny library in Pimlico, or go to an occasional film for sixpence, walking to the Chelsea Classic, or all the way to Victoria to see Deanna Durbin, or *Henry VIII* with Charles Laughton for a shilling, or *Marie-Antoinette* with Norma Shearer and Tyrone Power as an implausibly Swedish lover, and Tess doesn't understand how a queen can behave so.

Hold on, old lady, says John the psycho. Is the Houyhnhnm implying awareness and articulateness enough to defend mummy and quarrel about that? Putting on, perhaps, the beau rôle?

Perhaps. But no. The Houyhnhnm is trying to focalise the first conscious moment of deep divergence, ask the focus-puller. But right, mummy tells later, and the moment as remembered came at sixteen. But Tess was aware enough to keep quiet during the harangues. No idea now of the reasons for the quarrels. Judging by the later pattern, must have been against Joanne's bullying and constant interference. Once a quarrel is so violent Tess takes off a shoe and hits Joanne's shoulder, but Joanne grabs the shoe and bangs Tess's head till the blood flows. Joanne suddenly quietens and helps wash the head at the kitchen sink till the blood stops and clots. But there was a lot of complaining, an Easter holiday at Leigh-on-Sea for instance, presumably paid for by grandpère, and made miserable by Joanne's constant scorn about Leigh-on-Sea being a tripper's hole. And badgering mummy about going to Mass, never used to, popery is the religion of the poor.

Now and again the Smiths send the chauffeur in a huge

limousine, for lunch at the grand house in Esher. Diana has become very grand, very elegant. Mr Smith, rather large, is in armaments and Tess stares, half-remembering *Moral Rearmament*. So Mr Smith is responsible for those bombs on newsreels and indirectly for the young ladies' education and posh accent? Joanne loves these visits, opening rich vistas, Tess does not, and squirms. So, apparently, does mummy.

At the end of the second year at SSC, in 1938, mummy meets the train at the end of term as usual, and Tess first notices the grey hair, with a shock.

Clearly mummy is at wits' end about the girls' futures, meets a neighbour on the stairs, from the BBC, enjoins the girls to be nice, the man could be helpful. Tess gets a verruca on the foot and has to have an agonizing burn-out in several sessions with a chiropodist nearby. How about becoming a chiropodist, do ask, mummy urges. Tess has some school-snaps developed at the local chemist. How about photography? The habit Joanne so embarrassingly develops later, of pouncing on people imagined as useful, has a model, but with despair as cause.

That summer of 1938 Tess is sent to Germany, presumably at grandpère's expense, to stay with some German connection, Tante Emma, a baroness living in a Schloss near Ulm. Tess is fifteen. Joanne stays in London. Another mistake, but then Tess is taking German for School Certificate.

Tess travels alone, though put on the right train in Brussels by Tante Mathilde, and shares a second-class sleeper with strangers, a mere banquette, nothing like the grand wagon-lit to Carqueir-anne. When at last Ulm is announced the train goes immensely round the town like a long snake with a puffing plume tangential to the curve, and Tess sees the tallest cathedral in the world fluting elegantly upwards. Met by Tante Emma, a wide old lady, and driven in a light horse-carriage of sorts along a curving flat road towards, at last, a village hilled in woods surrounding the Schloss. The Schloss has a moat and a drawbridge. Tante Emma lives up winding stone stairs in a large and comfortable flat. Tess's room is enormous, as is the bed. Tante Emma is pleasant enough but severe, and takes Tess through *Wilhelm Tell* every day.

Tante Emma's daughter Gisele and son-in-law live in the flat below. There's a baby boy called Rainer, left crying for hours in a pram outside, good to pay no attention, make a man of the child. The whole family goes to the village church on Sundays, sitting in the baroness's pew above the villagers. The church is stark and Protestant. So these are the German people la Grande Guerre was all about.

The family is rigidly for the Führer (Führer of what? Sounds like girl guides again). The Führer is getting rid of the Jews. Tess thought the Jews were only in the Bible. Tess is made to listen to the speech of Herr Hitler on the radio and can't understand a word in all that fury, prefers Schiller. In Ulm, when friends are encountered and say Heil Hitler, Tess doesn't raise the arm but replies To Hell Hitler, swallowing the first T a bit just in case. But as a joke, out of a sense of the ridiculous, not from understanding. Tess is introduced to a girl Helga in Ulm, and goes visiting. The family lives on the Danube, grey and narrow here, and the girls walk along the river to where some other river, much greener, joins the grey. The waters hardly merge, no aquaescence here, how brave. Helga belongs to the Bund der Deutsche Mädel, and shows Tess photographs of a vast ceremony attended at Nüremberg last year, in a place like a huge sports stadium full of tall red and white flags Tess has also seen in Ulm, with a strange black sign in the middle. Tess enthuses politely.

One day Tess is taken to the Kino, and on the way out feels a violent pain in the right side, passes out, comes to and vomits in front of everyone. Rushed back to the castle, then back to Ulm for the hospital in the family doctor's car, every bump an agony. Acute peritonitis.

The doctor and the surgeon, a tall black-bearded man, stand on either side of the stretcher talking to Tante Emma. Tess is a minor and mummy's permission is required. Tess hears the words wird aber in einer Stunde sterben from the black beard. Operieren, operieren, Tess murmurs and passes out again. Tante Emma must have stood for parent. But after the operation the nurse leaves Tess for a few minutes with an open dressing and the wound gets infected, oozes pus, can't be sewn up again, so Tess has to just let heal under a bandage for months. The hideous scar is still there today. But then, the old lady's body is full of scars, operation-prone at periods when surgeons are clumsy still, increasing body-shame for years.

In the grand room where Tess is still in bed, convalescing, Tante Emma's son Gerd, home on a visit, comes in to tell Tess more about the Führer, such a good thing, the Anschluss, all Germans together, and how the Jews had crept into all the richest jobs and were running and ruining the country until Herr Hitler came, how Herr Hitler got rid of unemployment, building the magnificent Autobahns, all in English this time to make sure Tess understands. But Tess still doesn't, supposes an Autobahn is just a road for cars, but then, so are all roads. Gerd is thirty and handsome and bullish with thinning ash blond hair.

At last Tess is put on the train, still wonky, circling all round Ulm and the tall spire again, to Brussels. Jean-Luc is there, a young man of fourteen in long trousers, and both are photographed in the Parc de Woluwe, les petits fiancés, says Tante Mathilde, laughing. Here Tess is told about the crisis over the Sudetenland, wherever that is, but by the time London is reached the crisis has apparently gone away and there is Peace in our Time. Tess sees Disraeli and Peace with Honour.

This year the school receives two little girls from Germany, into the Junior school, two sisters, Jewish refugees. Joanne and Tess are no longer the only charity cases, nor the only foreign curiosities. Tess does, however, get an inkling of the German experience now, and of the strange world outside immediate Tess, careless with inklings. What were Tante Emma and Gerd trying to do, convert or justify? For once Tess didn't merge, kept a distance.

In June Joanne and Tess come out tied top in the school results, and are praised publicly at prayers as the best candidates in School Certificate, though that's not saying much, given the low standards of the school, where only one or two stay on for Higher. Tess is pleased by this equality. When the results come out in the papers, Tess has taken more subjects including maths and gets more distinctions, and Matriculation. But Joanne seems used to that by now.

The summer of 1939 is spent in Holbein House, and one morning mummy is bent over the newspaper. An aeroplane has crashed in the Vosges, killing all passengers and crew including the air-hostess Josette Blair, daughter of Oncle Walter. That stops Joanne's scenes for a while. Then grandpère dies, at seventy-seven. Mummy goes over, Joanne and Tess living on bread and butter and fruit. Mummy returns and tells about the shock at seeing the coffin vertical in the lift. Granny's was taken down by the stairs. Soon afterwards the Stalin-Hitler Pact is signed and mummy says Thank God grandpère didn't live to see that. As usual Tess doesn't understand. Tess understands little despite matriculation. Joanne understands more without. What a difference a year and another outlook can make. Remember the magazine L'URSS grandad used to get? Tess remembers only La Grande Ourse.

There are invitations from school friends. Joanne goes to stay with Joan Grey in Cookham Dean, Tess is invited by the prefect Janet Weston. Janet had belatedly taken Tess under a reforming wing before leaving, and is now doing a domestic science course. Though strikingly ugly with a long red face, piggy eyes, large mouth but golden hair, Janet is already engaged to Jock, a Classics schoolmaster in Windsor. Janet has two brothers, both at Marlborough. John sings *O for the Wings of a Dove* to Mrs Weston's accompaniment, imitating Ernest Lough but with a voice about to break. Peter, the elder, is Tess's age and looks like Janet but such looks seem less ugly on a boy, even handsome. For the first time Tess feels well dressed and shapely, conscious of Peter's glances, mummy having received a large case of rich give-away clothes from Mother St Paul, of Tyburn Convent, whatever that is. And one day Tess notices, for the first time, an elegant lady in Sloane Square, wearing a very short skirt, barely below the knee, like a schoolgirl. Like Tess. The inverse shock of seeing Joanne in a long skirt three years ago. Fashion changed last autumn, says Joanne. In preparation for war?

But mummy has made plans for the beginnings of the future. Joanne is to go to Stockholm to stay a year with Tante Vanna, but suddenly wins a scholarship to a fashion-school and decides to do that instead, to mummy's delight. That's one future settled. Better than serving at the counter in Boots, as constantly envisaged with horror. And Tess is to go, at sixteen, to teach English at a school in Rosenheim in Bavaria. Are Tante Emma and Gerd behind that? To leave on 3rd September. But first Tess is invited to stay with the Rice-Jones family on the Broads, to meet Roland, for Roland had the job last year. A young couple is also there and all four go out sailing, Tess showing total ignorance even of what baling is. The couple is necking in the boat, Tess sits rigid and embarrassed, Roland tactfully not touching but steering and talking about Rosenheim. In the evening Tess says yes to sight-reading madrigals à quatre, but all is politely stopped when the alto is heard to be all wrong. Madrigals aren't hymns. So much for Tess's awkward entry into society.

Tess does not go to Germany. Joanne does not go to Stockholm or even to the fashion-school, though why the war should stop that Tess can't think. There won't be any fashions in wartime, mummy says, but the headlines claim the war will be over in a few weeks. Surely mummy is being a little short-sighted? War-work, mummy says. Like last time. Mummy has silently sat for the Censorship exam in French and German and is being sent to Liverpool, at £4.10.0 a week, a fortune. And takes the girls along to a gloomy building in Westminster to sit the same exam, Joanne protesting all the way, and for once Tess is on Joanne's side. Why does mummy assume imitation without discussion? But Tess obeys as usual, takes the exam in French and German, Joanne in French, each upping ages, Joanne to eighteen and Tess to seventeen.

After the Chamberlain broadcast at eleven on September 3rd, the banks and shops in Sloane Square are suddenly hidden behind a wall of sandbags with a narrow entrance and a notice saying Business as Usual, the sirens wail sickly in a false alert, and Joanne starts up a great anti-bomb drama, refusing to stay in London, until at last mummy gives in and arranges for a lady near Worthing in Sussex (how has mummy come to know anyone at all in these three hard-working years?) to take the girls in until the results come through from the Censorship. Mummy goes off to Liverpool, closing the flat but paying the rent, just in case, and paying the lady in Sussex, thus trebling the expenses, but Joanne takes all that for granted and is calmed. There are no air-raids.

All the dominions and colonies one by one declare war, and

Tess is impressed, but wonders why all these people should come over and die in trenches because England guaranteed an unreachable Polish frontier.

By now Tess is reading at last, *Bleak House, Villette*, all about Brussels, and Shelley, Keats, Coleridge, Milton, done at school. Alone on the Sussex Downs, watching the sky still empty of aeroplanes, making the vow down the rabbit-hole. Joanne chiefly grumbles about the landlady.

At last the results arrive. Joanne has got in, being falsely eighteen, Tess is too young at falsely seventeen. Joanne is to go to the gloomy building in London and collect a ticket for Inverness. To read fishermen's mail, Joanne says mockingly.

Tess receives detailed instructions from mummy. Tess is to go with Joanne to Holbein House, and after Joanne's departure, repack the school trunk with all unneeded objects and a smaller case with minimum clothes, wait for the removers to come and take the trunk and the furniture and Joanne's upright piano into storage for the duration. And then to hand over the keys, to take a train from Euston to Liverpool Lime Street.

And Tess does everything, with immense pride at being considered so grown-up and responsible. With regret, Tess packs Pooh Bear, companion from Chiswick to Brussels to Folkestone, into the trunk. The life of billets and bedsits has begun. Tess will not develop a sense of owning objects or of belonging anywhere until much, much later, long after the war. But for the first time, Tess exists. Goodbye SW3, Farewell Sloane Square.

7. FILE: LIV'POOL

The Intercity from Euston to Liverpool Lime Street hurtles through the hoary fog towards a piece of past at a pace making the old lady nervous. The old lady has often taken the much faster French TGV though never in fog. But then, this is bifografy. The young man opposite has a black briefcase open on the tablette and makes non-stop calls about figures and facts on some fanion phone. So revising lecture-notes is disallowed.

The pace of change must have seemed swift to mummy's generation, but is now a TGV, anything old unrecognizable, mere relic, to the young, and inversely. Youth has so mutated since youth, since womanhood, middle-age and old age as to be a different species, with no future in the head the way people now old had a future and still have, in the head if not in real time. Girls of sixteen seen in the finals of Come Dancing look like grandes dames in masses of tulle and sleek hairdos in the arms of tall graceful gentlemen of nineteen in black tails and white tie. Boys of twenty or so play the Stock Exchange or do business deals by phone on trains, or hike across the world and get kidnapped or arrested for carrying drugs, boys learn to murder at ten and by eighteen die of overdose in the streets. Schoolgirls are young mothers, know all about drugs and condoms, though many more don't and drift. Divorce has become the norm. But even old men's memoirs are full of beastliness at school or war. The old lady can barely admit, let alone reconstruct, the retarded mental and physical age of Tess at sixteen, the ignorance, the innocence, the non-connecting of things, the permanent being elsewhere, not the elsewhere of religion or art or grand designs, but a haze, a fog.

The stations on the way, Rugby, Nuneaton, Stoke-on-Trent,

Crewe, are cleaner but otherwise the same, whereas Euston looked like an airport, with tiled floors and bright precincts and cleaners every few minutes, a tarted-up cry from the smeary stations of youth with piston-packing engines smelling of smoke and urine. The conservationists of steam engines romanticize on country lines. But London and other cities are less grimy since the Clean Air Act of the late fifties or Whenever.

Liverpool: the first job. And the Blitz. Curiously, the Liverpool Blitz is never mentioned in war history-books, only London and the Baedeker towns, Coventry, Exeter, Bath, Norwich. The Blitz was said to have been a convenient slum-clearing, yet today there are slums again, called inner cities. And high-rises. The Isle of Dogs in London now crouches below the vast skyscraper development of Canary Wharf, empty and bankrupt. Tess never saw real slums, in either Liverpool or London, except from trains. Nevertheless, the poor had slums to live in, nobody except tramps, romanticized by W.H. Davies, slept in the streets.

Runcorn at last, the bridge flanked by half-moons of crisscross metal, means Liverpool next stop. Soon the fanfaro phoner tells the fallopian tube the train is about to enter a tunnel and please ring back later. The old lady doesn't remember the tunnel but recognizes the chasm of red rock, the rock of old Chester, the rock of the new Liverpool cathedral, barely finished at the time. Eleven o'clock.

The old lady has told the host about wanting to visit the business centre of Liverpool before the talk at five, and David generously suggested an early train so as to drive around. The old lady steps out onto the platform, walks towards the station and gets a sudden shot of mummy in the long grey-green autumn-coat and small green hat hugging grey hair. But there's nobody there. A real film would have done such a flash in black and white, to suggest the period, whereas memory sees colours. David is a little late, no, the train is actually early. Lime Street Station is also light and clean but otherwise unchanged.

David takes the old lady on foot to the Adelphi Hotel nearby. The Adelphi! Tess would never have dared even to walk up the steps. The entrance-hall is huge and high and golden, the tea-hall beyond up golden stairs even huger and goldener. Strether came here off the boat and met Miss Gostrey, James's 'ficelle', at the counter by 'the lady in the glass cage'. But Tess didn't know about Strether then. There is still a lady in a glass cage, several, but no ficelle. Up in an ornate lift to the room, along high wide corridors papered in blue and yellow art nouveau, turning several corners to deposit the small case. Two splendid pink washstands, intermediary between Henry James and now, uselessly line the right wall, for clearly the bathroom on the left must have been added even later, bringing the big bed forward.

Outside again, Lewis's stands opposite, unrecognizably glassy and, on the right, the grand vista towards St George's Hall and the monumental public library beyond, where Tess borrowed Pierre Loti and Romain Rolland's *Jean Christophe* on mummy's enthusiastic recommendation, volume by volume, in a self-convince of loving the books as much as mummy did as a girl. But everything is pale gold, like Greek temples, instead of black.

As David drives, the old lady asks if The Bluecoat Chambers are still there, yes, and the bookshop Philip Son & Nephew, no, and the Philharmonic, yes. But there's no time. David is taking the old lady to lunch at the Anglican Cathedral, how odd. The trams are bright olive. A sign for Aigburth appears, ah, yes, Aigburth Road. But that would be too far, and uninteresting. There's a big parking around the red cathedral and a view over the city to the Mersey, and inside beyond the nave, a comely self-service restaurant called The Refectory.

After lunch, back down to the city. The traffic has been re-ordered round St George's Hall and the entrance to the Mersey Tunnel, making the huge space once crossed on foot or on a bike unrecognizable. David manages to park near Water Street, a prolongation of Dale Street to the docks. Water Street is very short, with only five large granite buildings on the right, opposite the India Building. The old lady examines each entrance to find the building Tess worked in. There was a side entrance on a cut corner, where Tess brought in the bicycle to take down to the basement before getting into the lift to the fifth floor. None of the five buildings has a corner entrance. Lloyds Bank House is still there, with the grandiose front-doors, and next to Lloyds another building, also with a central front entrance but, lower down, a cut corner. This might once have been a second entrance. For bicycled employees perhaps. Or all employees, not clients. But if this second entrance has been removed and walled over, there is no trace. And, in the mind, no memory of the number.

The old lady is stupidly disappointed. Why do places and events matter, so neutral to others, simply because lived? Alone the old lady would have looked again, inquired, had fantasized sailing up there and into the firm to say hello. But the old lady has entered a time-warp: if seventeen then and sixty-nine now, all those older colleagues would be retired if not dead, the time-span shrunk by memory shift yet expanded by the spendthrift real.

A walk down towards the docks. But there's a wide dual carriage-way crossing Water Street and access is impossible. There are no ships anyway. When arriving early Tess cycled on to the docks to watch the big ships and wonder about the world, the war, the wares. So David takes the old lady back up, through the ornate hall of the India Building to the car, to visit the Roman Catholic Cathedral, a mere deep dug site then, with half a crypt and grand white Byzantine plans, but now sitting on a hill like a concrete wigwam or a satellite launch. Nor was there such a view over Liverpool, streets and buildings stood close around the site. Now the two cathedrals face oecumenically on respective heights, one red, massive, mock-Gothic, the other white, modern and frail. But the interior is much more stunning, a theatre-in-the-round for nave and dark blue and red stained-glass effects everywhere.

That night, in the luxury room, after a gregarious Thai dinner nearby and plenty of wine, the old lady remembers the number: 5 Water Street. The number shakes up the name: Freedman, Paterson & Co. And the two directors, Mr Granville, tall and grey, Mr Paterson, short and swarthy. And several men in the big room, Mr Carver, and a younger podgy man Charlie Hedgerow, called Hedge, and Jack Plimsley, a severely acned or perhaps pocked young man with a horsy face and bulging grey eyes. Jack sat opposite Tess at a long wide desk and explained, in vain, why the cashbook account or the motor van account had to be posted to the ledger, that is, transferred inside out, item by item, inverting the debit and credit columns. The old lady checks the phone book, first under names, then under Accountants. There is no Freedman, Paterson & Co., no Granville, no Paterson, no Carver under Accountants, nor, for the younger ones, any sign of a C. Hedgerow or a J. Plimsley. Perhaps Charlie and Jack got killed in the war, or turned to higher things than accountancy. Now fragments and figments in the old lady's head, once human beings joked with daily.

The next morning the old lady hesitates before going on to Manchester, repeat performance, but plenty of time to walk down to Water Street again and see if that cut-angled building is number five, even to go up to the fifth floor and the big office with the grand client-counter. But lets go, buys a map of Liverpool and gets on an almost empty local train, much too early. As the train leaves Lime Street Station, the old lady unfolds the map to get back lost bearings. There is the long Aigburth Road, a thick yellow line to the South. And there, to the North East, in West Derby, at last, Broughton Hall, surrounded by a little park.

Lime Street Station. Tess steps off the train, carrying the small case. Mummy is waiting, slim and grey-haired under a velvet green hat, in the long coat of grey-green herring-bone worsted. Relieved, smiling, says Tess looks tired.

That's not surprising after a slow and sooty journey on the LMS. For years mummy will say in every circumstance Tess looks tired, or dishevelled, or badly dressed, never Tess looks nice, but Tess hasn't yet learned to resent this as absence of compliment, nor to decode as concern, rather than fact of life.

Liverpool seems cleaner than London, more like Brussels where every Friday every housewife or concierge had to scrub the pavement in front of the house, les gros derrières fleuris, according to grandpère. And there are trams, as in Brussels, no smelly red buses. The trams aren't yellow, though, but pale olive green and cream. The tram-journey is long, into the wide dual-carriageway called Aigburth Road. Ribbon-development, mummy says, all jerry-built, and Tess wonders how Germans came to build houses here, so different from those in Germany. With identical pebble-stuccoed half-houses stuck together, each a small double garden in front and back-garden and garage. Tess is impressed.

At Number 484 the Grant family has accepted Tess as co-billetee, sharing a creamy back room with two beds on the first floor, as well as the creamy front parlour, with a cream sweet, as Tess hears, of sofa and armchair round an open fire and a shiny black grand nobody plays, permanently shut under a vase of artificial flowers, though Tess is allowed to play before tea, without opening the top. Mr Grant is a builder, proud owner of a wheel-less car in the garage, laid off for the duration.

There is a daughter of sixteen, called Jean, short and plump with fluffy-chicken hair, more advanced in feminine wiles than Tess. Jean has a job already, at Rootes, whatever that is, and washes a unique pair of silk stockings every night in the bathroom but never takes a bath, much to mummy's amusement. In fact nobody takes a bath except mummy and Tess, rationed to five inches shared one after the other once a week, but a bath is luxury after Holbein House. There's a granny, never seen, in a small room on the first floor landing. The Grant couple have the front bedroom and Jean presumably an attic room. The billeting charge for lodging and food is one pound a week each. Supper is at six, called high tea, with bacon and eggs or sausages or fish and chips or kedgeree, never heard of but delicious. At ten Mrs Grant brings Horlicks and biscuits into the parlour, called supper. Tess has difficulty at first with Liverpudlian, and never catches the accent as had been feared for Cockney, but soon decodes the vowel equivalents. Adjusting to Liverpudlian is a bit like adjusting to bruxellois, and with the same warm lilt.

The first thing mummy does on arrival is to show Tess a letter from Inverness. Joanne's handwriting is huge and round, covering many pages, and expresses in uncurtained terms Joanne's fury at the bloody stupidity of giving up the flat in Holbein House. Joanne wants a roof after this idiotic war, any blithering idiot can see the war will be over in a few weeks, and so on, repetitively.

Joanne's just like daddy, mummy says furiously. Incapable of a thought for others. Had to be dragged to that Censorship exam and now at seventeen is earning the same salary. And out the anger pours, mummy's same salary covering Tess's keep and supposed to pay rent in London for untold weeks or months, more likely years if the last war's anything to go by. Inouï. Same in London, haranguing for money and clothes and holidays, scorning that very flat as a slum, criticising the family as bourgeois when the family was paying for SSC expenses. But daddy was at least charmingly devious, never vulgar. Look at the language! And the aggressiveness drowns the contradictions, even in the same sentence.

Mummy goes on like this for some time. Tess is silent. But this letter sows the seed of a first consciousness, dim and inexplicit still, of all being not well with Joanne. So far Tess has regarded the quarrels as other mere facts of life, and still retained an aquaescence to Joanne's superiority in all things except brain work, and an unthinking belief in sisters being friends, accepting differences, and being sometimes as complicit as twins. That sometime complicity breaks now, and will slowly, very slowly for there is little contact till after the war, turn into a totally mad, repulsive, compulsive correspondence over forty years, full of scorn and accusations accompanied by demands on Joanne's side, and, on Tess's, uneasy shifts from yielding to abject pleading to explaining to counter-attacking the constant carpings at Tess's way of life, as well as the battery-ramming of well-worn opinion as if eternal truth.

The letter is also the beginning of a fond association with mummy, almost a stranger before. At last living together, with-out grandparents or anyone, finding the same seriousness of pur-pose, the same humour, the same withdrawing instincts during the talking and mending or sewing every evening. Talking, though, is a façon de parler, for mummy has always expected Tess, if not Joanne, to agree with all the ideas mummy was brought up on, telling Tess a little about the family, about the humiliations in getting maintenance out of daddy, about the Other Woman, about the sudden freedom for women during the Grande Guerre, and the subsequent quasi status quo ante bellum, about Joanne's difficult character. Mummy never calls Tess Tess, but darling, and introduces Tess to the Grant family as Theresa, a strange new identity, a public role adopted from now on. Mummy never looks at Tess when talking but away into the room or down at the sewing, and never mentions religion, or sex. Nor is Tess interested.

Very soon a part-solution is found for Tess as financial burden: a call for trainees in *The Liverpool Echo*, and Tess is made to write in, as Theresa Blair-Hayley, as on the birth-certificate, as on the passport, yet never used so far, at school just Tess Hayley. Tess seems to have become a different person. A reply comes, followed by a trip together downtown, to a mail-advertising firm behind Lord Street. A genially persuasive boss explains how on payment of a modic sum, eight pounds, huge for mummy, Tess shall be taught shorthand-typing for three months, staying on three more months to work for the firm. Mummy signs the contract and forks out, delighted at this opening, dreams of a future in mail-advertising. Like daddy.

Oh? Was that daddy's business?

Yes. Daddy was director and in fact inventor of The Medical Addressograph Company.

Whatever's that?

Well, there were printing machines with the names of all the doctors in England, printing out envelopes to send news of recent medicines. A very new idea then.

Tess has never heard mummy express any kind of pride in daddy. But is bucked at being selected at all, and travels daily back and forth by tram, strapped like everyone with a gas mask in a cardboard box. These have to be protected by smart cases of oil-cloth or leather, bought in the shops. Tess is not, of course alone under tuition as imagined, but in a pool of girls each more Liverpudlian and giggly and friendly than the other. At lunch-time the girls go out in groups to a cheap canteen nearby, on the first floor above a shop, where a twopenny meat-pie can be got and a halfpenny cup of tea or, as Tess later tries to save for a three-and-sixpenny ticket to the Philharmonic, a penny fish cake and a cup of tea. Liv'pool is the first lesson in living.

Jean Grant is also a mentor in living, and knows all the hit-tunes. One is about the birth of a son to a Jones family, called Franklin D. Roosevelt Jones, and has a yesseree-yesseree refrain Tess mishears as kedgeree, kedgeree, kedgeree-ee-ee-ee-ee. Tess and Jean occasionally take the tram to town on Saturdays and go to the pictures, to see *Wuthering Heights* or Fred Astaire and Ginger Rogers in *The Story of Vernon and Irene Castle*, or James

Cagney in *Angels with Dirty Faces*, then go to the top floor in John Lewis's, a massive stone building like the Oxford Street shops, where there is a tey-dongsong, at only one-and-sixpence up in the rectangular gallery, to watch, not participate. Jean has a crush on the singer in a maroon suit singing *Begin the Beguine*, so Tess gets excited too, confusing the beguine with le béguin, French for crush or crackpot.

The Royal Oak is sunk at Scapa Flow, losing 800 men. The first war-drama near home. The Germans scuttle the Graf Spee in the River Plate after a lost battle with the Royal Navy. Whatever are the warships doing out there? 300 British prisoners taken from ships sunk by the Graf Spee are rescued from the tanker Altmark off Norway. Russia invades Finland. The British Expeditionary Force is in France hanging up washing on the Siegfried Line and telling the Germans to Run Rabbit Run. Lord Haw-Haw threatens on the wireless and knows everything. But apart from the gas masks and the blackout and the beginning of ration-books, Tess is not aware of being at war, for the dreaded air-raids haven't happened and there are no tranchées anywhere, now Britain and France have let Poland collapse between Germany and Russia. All action seems to be at sea, like battles in history-books. And despite watching mummy dramatic over headlines, Tess becomes even more withdrawn into a parallel world of woolly wonder and titillating trivia.

The winter of '39 is bitterly cold, with snow piled over a metre high along the streets. Tess hasn't seen such snow since Ciergnat. Mummy tries to inculcate some sort of clothes-sense, and after showing a firm distaste for the maroon craze in all the shops, takes Tess to Jaegers in Lord Street to buy a suit, in green and yellow check wool tight over the breasts, and Tess feels wretchedly ill-at-ease.

The group has done time in the typing class and joins some twenty girls in another larger room, addressing hundreds of buff envelopes all day, forgetting the shorthand learnt. Tess now understands the trick: one paid teacher, for eight pounds paid per girl, in exchange for an unlimited supply of forty unpaid typists. Tess thinks of daddy's machines. Mail-advertising is not for Tess. What is?

At the end of the contract Tess is sent to the Labour Exchange with a course-certificate. The Labour Exchange! Visions of long queues, no work, the dole, protest marches. But all that seems to have vanished. The woman hears the Southern accent and sees the matriculation, is impressed. Tess is pleased and grateful yet somehow not surprised, moving in a world where a book, pronounced boook, is a magazine, and feels well educated, with no notion of going further, or even of the possibility of going further, or of what a university is. Nobody in the family has been to a university, nor has a university ever been mentioned as existing, nor does mummy ever give a glimpse of future studies during evening talks or walks in Sefton Park. Just as well, since there's never been that sort of money.

Tess is sent to a firm of Chartered Accountants, whatever that is, called Freedman, Paterson & Co, in a grand modern building at 5 Water Street, with a palatial entrance, but has to go to another entrance on the corner lower down. The office is on the fifth floor and the marbled corridors go all the way round to swing doors and a large counter. A skimpy boy, but very self-assured, comes out from a switchboard cubicle on the left, then leads Tess through to a large office for an interview with an aged Mr Granville. Tess, thrilled, is to earn seventeen-and-sixpence a week! To operate the switchboard, Mr Granville explains kindly, as the two office-boys will be called up in a year or two. But after seeing Tess's terror-stricken eyes, or perhaps the matriculation, Mr Granville leads Tess into the larger room, with three long wide tables and large light windows full of sky and bits of buildings, and introduces Tess to a spotty young man called Plimsley. Plimsley places and opens out a Uriah Heap sized ledger on the desk and tells Tess to check the additions. Columns and columns, towers of dozening pennies to clamber down then race up again, down the scoring shillings, up again and down the piling pounds. Tess's shorthand, like so many later knowledges, slips off, though typing is like bicycling and remains, however unused.

Tess is slow at first, and Plimsley laughs. Plimsley laughs all the time, at Tess's posh accent and posh name. Tess is ignorant, not only of accountancy but of music-hall, of popular songs, of sexual innuendoes, always has a book to take to lunch, and walks into the office reading. Tess likes classical music and goes to the Philharmonic. Highbrow miss, Plimsley says, whatever that means. How strange, Jean Grant never mocks in this way. In fact, at seventeen, Tess is a semi-literate snob and a prig. But mockery is another fact of life, to be learnt, as are the grandeur of these offices and a ladies' cloakroom such as Tess has never seen, for even SSC had dingy bathrooms and loos. Tess looks into the glass: the brow does seem high, even bumpy.

Mummy is aux anges. A most respectable career, work hard at book-keeping and pass all the exams, only four years. Tess can't imagine four years. Mummy does not, however, suggest let alone arrange for Tess to take evening classes in book-keeping, assuming that, like God, the firm will dispense all. But perhaps mummy is secretly hoping Tess will marry young and need no job, no career, whereas Tess has equally secretly sworn not to marry at all, or, by way of contingent compromise, not to marry before twenty-eight. The time-space between is cottony, the vow on the Sussex Downs postponed for the duration. Tess as adder-upper learns very little.

One evening Plimsley offers to stay on in a small side-office and give Tess a lesson. From the point of view of the ledger, from the point of view of the motor van account, Plimsley repeats, and talks of stock in trade heard as stocking trade, but sits close and soon Tess feels an arm round the waist, pressing. An electric shock shoots through the bowels and Tess is paralysed, feels a hot blush mounting and takes in nothing. Very disagreeable. But soon bland Mr Carver takes Tess on audits, to read out endless figures from one book or a pile of invoices while Tess ticks off the same figures in another, or vice-versa, so there isn't even any adding, Mr Carver does that. The displacements are enjoyable, one day in a tailor's poky back-shop on high stools, another in the swanky boardroom of a Shipping Office. Tess sees Life.

The change of work coincides with a change of billet. Mummy has found another, as usual without telling, in West Derby, more convenient for Edgehill where the Censorship is lodged in a green glass building previously housing the football pools, whatever those were, a sort of water polo perhaps. And above all more congenial for the now firmly practised but still mysterious religion.

For Broughton Hall is a Catholic convent, in a huge and dark Victorian mansion and a huge park with a lake. A circular road leads up to a great porch. Inside the front hall and turning left there's an immensely long parqueted gallery, then right, up a grandiose square stone staircase to an assemblage of three rooms, two enormous and facing, the large bedroom looking out through ornately Gothic windows onto the front grounds, the large sitting-room onto the park, linked by a small unused bedroom looking onto the glass conservatory. The bathroom is across the landing, with the only mirror of the apartment. In Brussels there was a tiny glass in the vestibule, in Holbein House a small head-mirror in one bedroom, same at school above the washstands, and same at Aigburth Road. Tess has no visual sense of a whole body, except for hateful glimpses in shop windows or, more pleasing, school snaps still looking boyish and flat-chested.

The lighting is by two gas-mantles on the wall, and there's also an oil-lamp on the table, as in the farm at Lovatens. For breakfast and supper there's a long walk down the wide stairs and along the gallery to the other side of the entrance-hall and through a dark stone corridor to the kitchens, where the meals are served in a dismal dining-room under a statue of St Roch with a hole in the knee, by a shuffling silent lay woman called Louie. Louie also brings up the coal, and cleans. The nuns live beyond, invisible, save in the garden walking in twos, or in the chapel. Mummy still never speaks of religion, but indirectly Tess absorbs the pervasive if unpersuasive influence, starts going to Benediction on Sundays and falls in love with the Tantum ergo. Latin and Gregorian chant thoroughly distance the school hymns and unpoetic prayers starting Vouchsafe O Lord. The C of E veneer has been shed like an old shawl. In the evenings, by the gentle glow of the oil-lamp on the table, Tess reads *Jean Christophe* or writes reams of Keatsish verse in rhyming couplets, long romances about knights and damsels with red and black and golden flowing hair, instead of studying book-keeping.

In the Spring Marian Grey arrives, the mother of Joan Grey, from Cookham Dean, where Joanne went to stay. Marian occupies the small bedroom and all three share the large sitting-room. Mummy must have remained in touch, for Marian also works at the Censorship, and there are constant jokes about the long letters from German refugees to spread families, always starting Meine lieben Alle, since each member forwards to the next. Mummy buys Tess a second-hand bicycle for thirty shillings, to save on trams.

Then the real war starts, quite suddenly, on May 9th. Germany invades Denmark and Norway, and Holland on 10th, then Belgium. Tanks, soldiers as nuns fall from the sky under parachutes. Called the Blitzkrieg, though that word will later be shortened and applied only to the massive air-raids. Mummy's eyes are riveted to headlines and maps. The Chamberlain government falls, a national government, whatever that means, is formed under Winston Churchill, never heard of before but the headlines say WINSTON IS BACK. British and French troops are landed in Norway around Trondheim, but soon have to escape or surrender. All enemy aliens are interned. By the 28th of May Belgium and Holland are occupied and British troops are surrounded in North East France. On June 4th, the defeat of Dunkirk, turned into a miracle by thousands of boats and into a victory by Churchillian rhetoric. The German army has simply gone round the famous but incomplete Maginot Line in the Ardennes and by mid-June parades down the Champs Elysées. On 22nd France signs an armistice in the same railway coach near Compiègne where Foch received the German capitulation in 1918. Britain is now surrounded. Tess is flabberghastly aware of the war. Politics is suddenly simple, no need to understand Nazism or Fascism or Communism or any other ism: Hitler is evil and mad and the Germans are Huns. Moved to the teenage core by the fall of France, Tess sends a poem to General de Gaulle's office in London and is thrilled at getting a polite reply from a subaltern. The first rejection slip.

But life continues, to Tess's surprise. All three go on a brief holiday to North Wales. A long letter arrives from Oncle Francis, describing the escape as Swiss citizens from Brussels to Geneva. In July Janet marries Jock, ten years older, and Tess is invited to the wedding in London, somewhere near Victoria. Mummy makes the pointless sacrifice, to give Tess ideas perhaps, and Tess takes the train down again, staying in a small hotel nearby and feeling very grown-up, but nonplussed by the appearance of the bridegroom, short and bald and pink and spectacled, with a curly orange surround like a tonsure. Janet is tall and blond. Yet these two pink fair people Tess hardly knows are the start of a firm wartime friendship and will indirectly change Tess's life.

The raids on Southern airfields start, soon called The Battle of Britain, followed by the Blitz on London. Mummy takes Tess to the Lake District in September, a small cottage next to Dove Cottage in Grasmere, and Tess plunges into Wordsworth. There is another family sharing meals, so mummy speaks French to Tess, and after lunch Tess vanishes into the mountains for hours (where is the location manager?), returning late for supper then gushing up impressions in a tall cardboard-covered exercise-book. The war is far away again. In October Joan Grey comes to stay at Broughton Hall.

Suddenly all is changed again. Mummy, secretive as always, has decided to go to Belfast with Marian, to a newly set-up Censorship Centre. Joan is to remain with Tess in Broughton Hall, to follow the same secretarial course. Since Tess clearly can't live on seventeen-and-six a week, an account is opened at Lloyds, the big building next to No 5 Water Street, mummy will pay in the pound a week necessary for the billet, Tess's wages being pocket-money. Very generous. The first cheque-book. And drawing out one pound every Friday in the grand banking hall.

Joan sits hunched over big breasts, just as Tess does, but is much more lethargic. At school Joan was always either painting black palm-trees in china ink against gorgeous watercolour sunsets, or reading the Brontës, Jane Austen and other authors Tess had never heard of, scorning games and all physical activities such as the dancing of tangos and foxtrots after supper in the Senior Common Room. Joan now raves about Margaret Irwin's historical novels and makes Tess read one about Rupert of the Rhine, and Axel Munthe's *Story of San Michele*, as usual incomprehensible. Joan's accent is artificially refined. A far worse cultural snob than Tess seems to Plimsley, bewailing this exile from civilization, scorning the Liverpool accent, subhuman, and the ignorance of the girls at work. So lowbrow, intolerable, and

Tess suddenly understands the distinction, but not the scorn. The genevois have an accent, the vaudois have an accent, the bruxellois have an accent, what's so terrible about a Liverpool accent?

Oh, so hideously wrong, not the King's English.

Tess doesn't see what's wrong. At least all the continental vowels are kept. The South of England is the only area in the whole of Europe where *i* is pronounced as *ai* and *a* as *ey* and *u* as *a*. Surely that's an accent too? And Keats spoke Cockney.

Joan is not impressed. Oh, for a beaker full of the warm South, quoted incessantly, though Folkestone in winter was hardly warm. In fact, Tess likes Liverpool, clear and airy and sane, at least the bits Tess cycles through. But Joan does open Tess to activities previously unknown, showing Tess a reproduction of Stanley Spencer's people resurrecting in Cookham churchyard. Tess finds the painting crude but daren't say so. Joan pores over art books, Fra Angelico, Filippo Lippi, El Greco, and is mad about Paul Nash. A new world. Apart from school excursions to Bruges and a memorable Memling the children stand around and gape at, there is little feeling for art at l'avenue de l'Opale, only some dark muddy paintings of Rhine castles in the hall, although grandpère is supposed to have once sculpted and painted. Joanne's talent is recognized and encouraged, and in London there was a dazed visit with Joanne to the Tate Gallery, but there stop Tess's notions.

For Tess spends all free time in Philip Son & Nephew, gazing at books too expensive to buy and incomprehensible when opened for a peep, *Absalom! Absalom!* or *Finnegans Wake* on the recently out display. But now saves pennies for weeks to buy the first ever book, still possessed, an art-book of El Greco, with coloured plates, a fortune at ten-and-sixpence. And a book of modern verse for five shillings. Under Joan's enthusiasm Tess discovers Hopkins, Whitman, Eliot. The girls go to exhibitions at the Bluecoat Chambers and the Walker Art Gallery. Tess counters the influence by persuading Joan to share the trances at the Liverpool Philharmonic, reading programme notes assiduously and getting girlishly excited by the visits of Malcolm Sargent or Myra Hesse, Eileen Joyce, and Moiseivitch, bearding these to the green room for autographs. And Joan counter-persuades Tess to the local rep to see Robert Donat in *Goodbye Mr Chips* and *Swan Lake* by the Polish Ballet Company. Tess forgets the religious inklings for Art. And so the modest education begins, through the winter of 1940-41, away from the London bombs.

8. FILE: WARWORK

Tess is reminded of the war when Roland Rice-Jones docks in Liverpool and calls for Tess at the office as a naval officer, much impressing the boys. Roland is in submarines and Tess shudders with imagined claustrophobia. Now Tess can laugh about the madrigals and talk of music, Roland defending Wagner, to Tess's surprise. Tess once heard the Tannhäuser Overture at the Philharmonic and decided to hate Wagner.

Tess is reminded of the war again when a gentleman calls at Broughton Hall for questions in the big gallery. Does Mrs Blair-Hayley work in the Censorship, in Belfast? Was Miss Blair-Hayley in the Lake District with Mrs Blair-Hayley last September? Did Miss Blair-Hayley write things down in a big book, and speak a foreign language?

So the family lodged with reported the French-speaking mother and daughter as Fifth Columnists. Tess is so amazed, so amused, so young, the gentleman laughs too and goes away satisfied. But Tess is also impressed. That's the way real spies are caught.

In February a German Korps lands in Tripoli to help out the Italians against Wavell. The Japanese are advancing everywhere in the Far East. The war is spreading further and further, a world war in a truer sense than La Grande Guerre. A novelist called Virginia Woolf commits suicide by drowning. Joan of course knows all about Virginia Woolf. At Christmas both travel all night on a freezing boat to visit the mothers in darkly massive Belfast, in a much more austere Catholic convent than Broughton Hall, with horrid cubicles. Mummy says Catholics are treated like underdogs by the Protestants. At Easter Tess travels down to London again, to stay with Janet and Jock in Windsor. Despite train-games with Jean-Luc Tess always hated real trains, but wartime journeys have become ten times worse, full of troops, no seats, and very slow. On every platform soldiers are kissing girl-friends or wives in uncomfortable-looking cinema-clinches, girl thrown back on one arm. Surely films can't be influencing the real? But then, Tess has never been kissed or seen grown-ups kiss.

Jock is now an Air Force officer at the Air Ministry in Aldwych, where Tess calls. Jock has a special allocation of petrol coupons and drives up and down from Windsor every day. This seems incredible, nobody Tess knows drives a car, and cars anyway are few, only taxis.

Isn't reading on the train more comfortable?

What, these days? Thinking in a car is even better, and not needing to talk to strangers.

Sorry.

Don't be silly. Besides, there's no Blitz in Windsor, unless by mistake.

For the first time Tess sees bomb-damage, and then the ribbon-development followed by regiments of low colourful buildings on the way out of London. What are those?

Those are modern light industries, Jock explains in a prim and precise speech. Nice and clean, unlike the big factories in the North. Light industries make soap, or breakfast cereals, or biscuits, as can be seen from the names.

Clearly Jock enjoys Tess's abysmal ignorance, a real school-master. Tess admires the beams on a pub and Jock pounces, that's mock-Tudor, twentieth-century, lower middle-class, and points out a real Elizabethan manor in the distance later on. Tess can't see any difference, except there are more beams. Jock is now on leave, and will use that to fill in a five-year gap in knowledge of the seventeenth century, and Tess is aghast. Entire centuries are gaps, except, gapfully, the nineteenth, done at school. Rashly Tess claims to adore the seventeenth century.

Oh, yes? What, particularly?

Well. Rupert of the Rhine.

Ah. Margaret Irwin.

The flat in Windsor is lined with books to the ceilings, every period and language from ancient Greek to modern times. Janet says proudly, Jock has read every single book. Janet has gone through this super domestic science course before marrying, and is a perfect cook, magical with meagre rations, perfect housewife, perfect wife, and this obviously suits Jock. Both are perfect in ways Tess never will be. But vistas are set ajar. Jock's delightful ancient mother has a grace-and-favour flat in Windsor Castle, up in a fat tower, and is very friendly.

Tess has now turned eighteen and could join up. Jock advises the Women's Auxiliary Air Force, the WAAF. Tess is thinking rather of the Land Army. Tante Dora was in the Land Army last war.

Nonsense, an intelligent girl, tilling fields in gumboots in all weathers and tending cows in dung.

Tess preciously retains the compliment.

The German occupation of Europe has spread South East into Hungary and Rumania through diplomatic pressures, followed by a military sweep through Yugoslavia to Greece, again to rescue the Italians. The British land troops in Greece but are swiftly ousted, and ousted again later from Crete.

Meanwhile the Blitz on Liverpool begins in May, shorter but as brutal as the continuing London Blitz. Joan and Tess refuse to go down into the cellars of Broughton Hall, declaring to Louie and the nuns, better to die in bed than under a crumbling manor. In fact the girls don't stay in bed but gaze at the searchlights and the flares and glares and flashes out of the tall Gothic windows, cringing and wingeing at the whistles and gunfire and heavy crunches, watching as spectacle the bombs so feared on film in newsreels. But Lewis's is in ruins, Lord Street is hit, and all the way down to the city Tess cycles past blocks reduced to piles of rubble half framed in weirdly standing walls with open rooms like shelves. A baby's arm juts out of the rubble. Or a doll's? Tess doesn't stop to look.

So Tess joins up, to escape not the Blitz, for that is now every-where, but accountancy, and is soon called to a training camp near Gloucester. The farewells at Freedman, Paterson & Co are unsentimental on both sides. Mr Granville is no doubt annoyed because Tess will not replace the office boys, on the contrary,

Tess volunteers before these are called up. Joan is to join mummy and Marian in Belfast, in the Censorship, and so is Joanne, how odd, transferring from Inverness. Mummy and Marian have, secretly as usual, rented a bungalow in the Northern suburbs. Joanne's turn to live with mummy. And mummy has great hopes, surely such a normal home-life will soften Joanne a little.

Tess gives away all clothes, except what's needed to travel in, to the convent, and leaves the bicycle and the one precious art-book in the nuns' keeping for the duration. Thus unballasted, except for the book of verse, Tess takes the tram downtown and makes for Lime Street Station once again, no doubt for the last time.

Tess had that thought and the thought was wrong. The Houyhnhnm chortles and neighs, happy to exist for a moment in two dimensions.

Cheater, says John[56], the script consultant, anyone can attribute thoughts in remake.

No, says the Houyhnhnm, Tess had all the thoughts attributed. The gaps are more difficult, the thoughts had and hopped.

Trillions and trillions, total recall, quelle barbe!

Et que le méchant loupe.

Loupe away then.

The brain's diskettes are worn away, the files won't come up in any detail. Four years of bytes in a churning of turning-points.

Barracks, uniforms again, not brown or blue or green but grey-blue, kitbags, military gas masks with corrugated elephant-trunks folded into shoulder-strap khaki holders. To learn, what? Marching in step, eyes right, salute, halt, stand at ease. Like boarding-school without the sport, the snobbery, the sanctity other than Saluting an Officer is not saluting the person but the King's Commission. Not prayers to images but a sort of diminished god.

Interviews, matriculation again a sesame, to Thornaby-on-Tees, North Yorkshire, at first in a genuine slum, Tess occupying the only bedroom and the entire family apparently sleeping in the grimy kitchen, then, thankfully, in barracks. Thornaby is a Coastal Command station, the ops room in a trapeze-shaped bunker with a cement corridor leading into an ante-room where the pilots are briefed, separated by a glass partition from the ops room with the high wall map of the East Coast, the North Sea, and Norway. The CO and Second have red and green phones on the long desk facing the map and Tess marches into a small cubby-hole on the right after smartly saluting. The CO calls out Blair...Hayley now and then, with a self-conscious smile at this peculiar regulation. Sir! A corporal climbs on a movable ladder shifting ships and planes over the map with a rod. The work is clerical, filling in and filing chits with plane numbers, departures and expected times of arrival, wind forces and speeds and heights. Tess learns the harbours and airfields down both coasts, the makes and parts of aeroplanes, called aircraft anyway, elements of meteorology and, with the corporal, how to calculate the triangle of velocity. Sometimes an aircraft doesn't return, perhaps a pilot Tess drank with in Stockton-on-Tees.

Tess discovers a small hut called the Education Office, with a few books. The Education Officer, a Flight Lieutenant with a ginger moustache, asks Tess to give German lessons to the Bomb Disposal boys. Hitch-hiking all over Yorkshire and Durham and Southern Scotland on forty-eight hour passes and leaves. Truck-drivers are friendly and respectful, sexual harassment unheard of then, at least by Tess.

The first leave is to Belfast, via Liverpool again, to the not so happy family in the bungalow, the Waaf outfit much admired. Joanne may be envious and not long after joins the Wrens, one-up as Senior Service, still in Censorship. Joanne is also furious about a naval officer showing great interest in Tess, unreturned, at a naval party in some castle on Lough Neagh. But Tess doesn't care, is only here on leave, is now no longer a burden on mummy, life is fun.

Suddenly, in early October, Tess is summoned by the Waaf CO, Section Officer Stevenson. What has Tess done? But fears land safely. The CO, a pleasant lady around forty, questions Tess about the German lessons and decides to recommend a commission. The King's Commission! Being saluted by Other Ranks! SSC had not managed to inculcate the desire for meaningless badges, nor was Tess ever a prefect, but is now impressed. Tess is still only eighteen, and seems to be having a good war.

Everything happens very fast, the new uniform at a Stockton tailor, on credit out of future pay, a much better fit than the dole-outs, with a half-stripe on the wrist as ASO, Assistant Section Officer, the long grey-blue greatcoat with epaulettes, half-belt and wide pleat at the back, Tess has not felt so advantaged since the box of Tyburn clothes three years ago, soon grown out of. But whatever Tess learns at the Cadet School in Loughborough, in the bitter cold of November '41, about rank and responsibility, is obliterated by the sequel.

For Tess is called to a London interview in a dark building behind St James Street with a flabby Wing-Commander Hampton and a handsomer Group-Captain Winterbotham, all in German. The Wing Commander hands out a long paragraph pasted on cardboard for Tess to translate, full of unknown technical terms. One of these is Klappenschrank, a word not found in any dictionary since. Tess struggles through, guessing, stumbling only over Klappenschrank, admitting defeat. The Wing-Commander kindly explains: a Klappenschrank is a flap on a field-telephone. Tess is given a railway voucher, first-class now, and told to go to Euston tomorrow for the next train to Bletchley, Bucks, and there to ask for Bletchley Park.

Bletchley Park. A check-point, a road to a red late Victorian mansion, all in length, on the left, a grey cement tennis-court beyond, lawns and trees and a lake to the right. Opposite the tennis-court is a long low wooden hut painted greyish white and, at right angles to that, the end entrance to another greyish hut, parallel to the first but further on. Hut 3. Inside, a narrow corridor with small offices on either side and a rattling noise. One door is open on civilian girls round a big grey machine doing the rattling. Tess asks for Wing-Commander Hampton. Down the corridor and turn right. The hut is right-angled. On the outside corner a roomful of army officers, on the inside corner a room with officers and civilians working at a round table. After the corner the corridor leads into a long wide room, with girls on the right in civvies, working at several tables covered with long boxes. Beyond these, several desks along the windows facing the other hut inside the angle. On the left, a vast wall covered with maps. Wing-Commander Hampton sits at one of the desks and at once introduces Tess to a pale girl in shabby civilian clothes, with witty grey eyes, a crumpled face and mousy hair drawn back but wisping down. Jane Shields. Jane'll explain everything, the Wing-Commander says and sits down again as a green phone rings. Winterbotham? Ready to scramble?

Tess had expected an RAF station, and here are civilians, air force and army officers all mixed up.

Jane Shields starts explaining. Look at this.

Tess gazes at a long piece of paper with mauve print.

A teleprint, or TP, one of the hundreds a day sent to Whitehall. See, the reference at the top is CX/MSS, with a number. MSS would mislead the enemy as meaning Manuscripts, but in fact stands for Most Secret Source.

Tess reads: Source found the following dispatch in a waste-paper basket.

The message is from OKW, says Janet.

What's that?

Oberkommando der Wehrmacht. Addressed to Field Marshal Kesselring, head of Luftflotte 2. Here, look on the map, Central Front, in Russia, with Heeresgruppe B. Kesselring is to transfer the entire Luftflotte to Sicily and become C in C Med. Dated 29th November '41, that's yesterday.

But the message is in English!

Of course. The boys on the Watch translate all the messages.

But how do – ?

All German signals are intercepted, well, not all, not those sent by landline in Germany and France, but all those sent over the air in operational areas. The Germans encode on a very special machine called Enigma, supposed to be unbreakable, but reconstructed from interception by Polish mathematicians in the thirties, and handed over to British officers in France just before Poland collapsed. The keys change every day but the system is known. The Enigma encoder's been complicated since of course, but the cryptographers break quite a lot every day, especially the general Luftwaffe key, called Red here. Well, not every day, and not every key, and not always on the day, but more and more often.

The crip what?

The cryptographers in Hut 6. There's a vast machine called the Bombe, or rather several, scattered over the area to avoid sudden destruction. The Bombe can try out thousands of possible cribs in minutes. Look, that's Hut 6 out there, and the hatch to Hut 3. All the decoded messages come through that hatch to the Watch. Come and see.

Jane takes Tess to the Watch, the square room in the angle of the corridor, with a large semi-circular horseshoe table and men in uniform or civvies sitting round the table facing a young man at the centre, in civvies, with curly brown hair and glasses. This is Bob Marshall, as Bob shakes hands and says There's a lull, and shows a few messages.

These are like telegrams, on rough buff paper with strips of five-letter groups pasted on.

Surprise surprise, says Bob, but this is decoded German. Has to be emended though, look.

Bob takes a message and a pencil and rapidly draws vertical strokes between certain letters, occasionally through a letter, putting in another above. Slight corruption, Bob explains, often much worse. Magically, once the five-letter groups are redivided and linked, the message becomes German: EINSA TZBER EITSC HAFTS MELDU NGNOV EMBER DREIS SIG and so on.

Don't worry, says Jane seeing Tess look terrified. Only the Watchboys do that, know German like English, plus the jargon.

Tess gazes at this clever boy with respect.

After emendation, Bob goes on, translation, checking by the head of the Watch (Bob looks down modestly), and comment when necessary from air and army advisers, then through the hatch to the Duty Officer next door for a final check, then to the teleprincesses to be sent up to Whitehall and commanders in the field. Ah, here's another batch, sorry.

The batch is distributed to the men around the table. By the inner hatch to the Duty Officer sit two other officers, one RAF one Army. The air and military advisers, Jane says on the way out.

Back in the big room, Jane stops at the tables with the long boxes.

This is the Air Index. The Army Index is in another room.

Tess is introduced to the head of the shift, a girl with lank strawberry blond hair and a round pretty face, called Jean Stelling. Behind Jean is another hatch, from the Watch. A head pokes through to ask for information. Another girl obligingly looks up a card in one of the long boxes.

Cheeky bastard, says Jean, supposed to come round and do the looking up. There's so much to get onto the cards, non-stop.

Jane Shields takes Tess to the Fusion Room, opposite the Index, packed with army officers and sergeants working on WTI.

What's WTI?

Wireless Telegraph Intelligence. Part of MI8. Frequencies and call-signs give a lot of information. Also called Y, at least the intercept stations are called Y-stations. All these terms'll become second-nature.

The walls are covered with star-designs done in coloured string and pins. But the room is too crowded, nobody can stop to explain.

Tess is to assist Jane Shields and sits at the same desk reading TPs and letters from AI.1(c) or whatever, and files. Jane is patient, and chatty about working for a London degree by correspondence course in whatever spare time is left.

What's a London degree?

Jane looks astonished. London University. Beyond Higher School Certificate, that was last year. In economics.

One or two girls at SSC stayed on for Higher, but Tess never inquired why or what. The measly matriculation, the so-far sesame, sinks into subsignificance. No wonder Jane looks tired and crumpled. But Tess is at once fired to do the same, and asks for details. The Americans come into the war after Pearl Harbor.

Tess doesn't work long with Jane, for the Wing-Commander and Jane soon vanish into a separate office, and Tess is now on the Index, transferring every item marked in pink on every TP by the head of the shift. Every Feldwebel posted to another unit gets a card with the name and rank, unit and destination, another for the unit left, another for the new destination. Together with the CX/MSS reference and date. Like people not counting in history-lessons, just armies moved on maps. Tess wonders whether some German girl is indexing Blair-Hayley, aircraft-

105

woman, from Gloucester to Thornaby-on-Tees, ASO, Cadet School Loughborough, Bletchley Park. But there's also much more important stuff, the daily strength-returns from everywhere, so similar as to make useful cribs, details of fuel supplies, railway movements, operational orders and reports, reports about the state of the German economy or heavy water in Norway, whatever that is, or mysterious allusions to a secret weapon preparing at Peenemunde, and from Russia (though scarce, because the distance of the radio-stations makes the traffic often inaudible), the Balkans, Norway, North Africa, Italy. All this also includes army and navy information coming on the Luftwaffe keys, for the Luftwaffe is intimately involved with convoys. And just as well, for the army and navy keys are harder to break, the Heer and the Kriegsmarine being much more disciplined about obeying all the procedural rules for the Enigma machine than the Luftwaffe. The army keys have bird-names, Gannet in Norway, Vulture and Kestrel in Russia, Chaffinch for Panzer Korps Afrika, but that's a tough key still. The Naval section is in Hut 8 and Hut 4, but naval keys are even harder, except for one called Dolphin. Japanese is dealt with in yet another hut, so although the Japs are sweeping South and both Hong Kong and Singapore have fallen, the whole attention in Hut 3 is riveted to German forces.

Tess has a pleasant billet, and of course enrols for Higher School Certificate in English, History, Latin and French, ordering books from Foyles and working every spare hour on early British history or Ovid's *Metamorphoses*, Book I. Jock approves. Tess now spends leaves with Jock and Janet as substitute parents and Jock opens many gates, even politics, simplifying socialism for Tess as taxing the rich to help the poor, splendid idea, very Robin Hood. In earlier periods the poor were taxed to help the rich. And Spring is here. Tess sends for the bicycle and rides to the Park along an empty back-road with Charles Oman's *England before the Norman Conquest* propped up on the basket.

Tess's mind is a maze, Proteus, Agricola threatening Ireland, Jagdgeschwader 27 moving to Africa. Indexing is mechanical, and Tess becomes familiar with individual units, types of reports and orders, but can't grasp the whole, can't bear not to grasp the

106

whole, so works overtime, poring over cards, taking notes, and finally makes an enormous chart on a roll of white paper, with every chain of command from OKW through OKH, the huge Oberkommando des Heeres, and OKL, through the five Heeres-gruppen (four? six? kept changing names at this stage) and seventeen Armies and five Panzer Armies , innumerable divisions and regiments, and the five Luftflotten, the Korps and Fliegerkorps and all the Geschwader and Staffeln down to the smallest Abteilung, and where operating. Jean Stelling is impressed, tacks the chart on the wall, everyone comes to look, why did nobody think of that before? Tess bathes in admiration, starts enjoying the work and understanding things. Mastering things.

Indeed, says John[53], another nasty piece of perk, the floor-manager perhaps.

In deed and in fact. For BP is Tess's first training of the mind, a first university. Tess learns the mysteries of accumulating apparently unrelated items to be redistributed on different cards for use. A piece of text can be analysed in the light of other information, every item noted to build up a vast powerhouse of knowledge and further clues for the advisers to interpret incomprehensible fragments. Tess also knows how sometimes action is not taken on important evidence in order to protect the source. Tess acquires a reverence for knowledge, tinged with the absolute secrecy and pleasurable guilt (Is intercepting Fair Play? Apparently the question was asked during the First War), but also glee, soon transformed into an awareness of the power knowledge gives. This particular knowledge too, comes out of the air, intercepted, decrypted, translated, transmitted, like the poetry Tess still sometimes finds time to write, listening to a silent voice, capturing, translating hazy notions and sharp impulses into words and rhythms. And Tess is surrounded by German scholars and mathematical brains with hobbies like ornithology or chess or Lieder singing, and becomes brutally aware of the highbrow culture supposedly possessed in Liverpool having been abysmally itsybitsy.

This can't happen all at once, says the nasty piece of perk, the old Houyhnhnm is hindsightly.

Knowledge is always useful at the time, says the old Houyhn-

107

hnm, often for reasons not clear then. Reading the whole war, for example, every day, from the enemy viewpoint, the British being the enemy, like the hysterical sympathy with the enemy felt by soldiers suffering in the trenches. The writer does that, learning to imagine the other. All human beings should, in fact, but don't always. On the other hand, experiencing that same war as pure information on teleprints, index-cards and maps, well-protected in the peaceful Buckinghamshire countryside, helps to turn Tess into a detached intellectual, never experiencing the grime, the cold, the heat, the suffering, the corpses, the land-mines, the tanks, except anodyned in newsreels. Tess's present notion of war is still derived entirely from postwar films. Suddenly aware then of having been complicitous in war, in male history. Like most women.

Tess also learns not to believe a word the papers or the wireless say, and out of fear of being unable to distinguish inside from outside information stops reading the papers altogether, so as to be sure everything known is secret. The gap is especially flagrant with the unreal newsreels, ludicrously cheerful and irrelevant when everything is going so badly.

Well, well, says the ironic John, why not step out of that ironic superiority and return to the abysmally itsybitsy?

The power of knowledge, the Houyhnhnm murmurs dreamily. But only when backed by imagination, competence and strength. Knowledge alone isn't enough. For Tess also learns, not from the immediate work but from talk among the Watch officers consulting the Index, or from Flight Lieutenant Jim Hardy asking Tess for help on a bit of back-research and chatting, of many bunglings higher up, and much dissension between Whitehall departments. Nobody is supposed to know more than the immediate work, for security reasons, but items filter down. The list of people entitled to receive Ultra, as the stuff is called up there, is very restricted still, and information isn't always believed. The Foreign Office, to Tess's amazement and despite numerous FO staff here, does not have access to military information, only to the diplomatic ciphers dealt with in the Main Building. Jim tells Tess how Whitehall long required BP to do no interpreting but to send the stuff raw. Total nonsense, says Jim, since the stuff raw often makes no sense at all. But BP won on that early. The Admiralty handles everything separately. MI6 and Air Intelligence are also constantly at loggerdunderheads. The joint work done in Hut 3, echoing the Luftwaffe's close involvement with Army and Navy, will take a long time to emerge higher up. And often the staff here are furious when MSS information has been ignored or reinterpreted, with severe losses. Something of the kind in fact happens soon after Tess's arrival. Hut 3 warn Whitehall and the Admiralty of faint indications on the main Luftwaffe key: the Scharnhorst, the Gneisenau and the Prinz Eugen may be about to break out of Brest and make a dash through the Channel to the North Sea, but the Naval Enigma settings for those crucial days in February were not solved till three days later, so the Admiralty has ignored Hut 3 and the warships pass safely.

These intimations are only echoes, at Tess's lowly level, and mostly Tess believes in the hundred percent efficiency of everyone above Tess. At school the follies of men, the muddling through, the someone had blundered, were taught as past, implying progress since to a modernly perfect present. But the intimations are confirmed in memory-wrenching detail fifty years later when the old lady, after eighteen years of silence followed by a long refusal to want to remember, finally starts reading the books now allowed about Ultra over the last two decades.

Itsybitsy please, says John the perk, the focus-puller.

9. FILE: LOVENWAR

A note from a Jonathan Hatter in the pigeon-hole, mad as a hatter
the note says, invites Tess to coffee. Jonathan Hatter has seen
Tess cycling to work reading a book on a basket, how daring, and
is all the more delected to discover the book is mediaeval history.
Jonathan is a lecturer in Mediaeval German at London University,
with a porous pale-mud face and pasty pale-mud hair, and the
two now spend hours bicycling along the carless roads and sitting
in solitary fields under summer trees with Tristan, Siegfried,
Parzifal and the Minnesang. Tess at once decides to become a
mediaevalist one day. All this and Ovid too take up all of Tess's
free time, as well as long strange novels as gifts, *The Tale of Genji*,
and *Orlando*, by Virginia Woolf, the drowned lady of last year.
Jonathan is married, with a small daughter, dreams of that daugh-
ter growing up to look beautiful playing the harp.

Jock continues to approve, sends back Tess's sub-Hopkinsian
poems saying only a dazzling technique, Tess has nothing to say.
But why should Tess-that-young have anything to say? Why
should Tess-that-young not learn the craft?

Such paterironizing, says John the piece of perk, by the abolishers
of Tess's discourse, the mentors, will fog the girl's frays and
phrases for years.

But Jock also helps Tess with extra Latin exercises, returning
corrections with added words about a big stick for errors and a
little drawing of a cane.

And Tess doesn't decode that at all, says the perk, until several
years later, when Janet and Jock, still childless, tell Tess about
Jock's impotence and tendencies. Used to put in that stuff about
the cane in vague hope, Jock will say disarmingly.

In fact Tess doesn't decode anything, certainly not Jonathan's increasing intensity and number of little notes with jocular glosses on Middle High German, and the friendship ends when Tess innocently writes an imitation letter to Jonathan at home on leave. Jonathan is furious. Jonathan has a wife. Well, Tess knew this, and can't understand why such a stimulating pastime on war duty has to be kept secret.

Mummy arrives, unhappy in Belfast. Joanne is now in the Wrens, somewhere in London, Marian Grey is going to the Foreign Office, Joan too. So Tess sent an application-form, amazed at the ease and at the reversal of aid. Mummy works in the Main Building, presumably on diplomatic stuff.

Nobody talks about work at BP, in fact the majority of people there are on peripheral work and not in the know, billeting officers and other admin staff, nurses and doctors, cooks, cleaners, wastepaper collectors for the fiery furnace, messengers, machine-operators, people working on minor ciphers, drivers to and from billets, dispatch-riders. With about a hundred men and women in Hut 3, and the same in other Enigma huts, there can't be more than some eight hundred persons in the secret. But peripheral awareness and not knowing the importance of the secret can be far more dangerous, and the old lady is still astonished at the way the Germans never suspected, nobody ever talked, either outside or inside, on the lawns, in the beer-hut, in the canteen.

Mother and daughter don't meet much anyway, except for an occasional lunch, but go to London to see Tante Vanna, suddenly arrived from Stockholm after two years of trying. Oncle André works for the Free French and is grumpy as usual, Tante Vanna is elegant as remembered from Brussels but with greying hair, and is hoping for a job in the BBC French section. The reunion is excited, telling of the efforts, the dangerous journey, and how Vanna's occupation as a diplomat's wife was written down as Unpaid Domestic. There is news of the family in Geneva. Oncle Francis is working for the Red Cross and Jean-Luc is studying physics in Zurich. But then, Tess reflects, Jean-Luc's education was always a cut above. At last a University man in the family.

Rommel has driven the British back across Tripolitania and Cyrenaica almost to the Egyptian frontier, helplessly followed by Hut 3 on a new army key called Scorpion and on Chaffinch, now read regularly. General Alexander takes over from Auchinleck as C in C Middle East, with a General Montgomery as Commander of the Eighth Army. Four days later a signal from Panzer Heer is decrypted forbidding reconnaissance near the Qattara depression so as not to arouse enemy suspicion, and in the next half hour another from Rommel to OKH and OKW, giving the complete plan for attack. Panzer Heer's situation has been critical since the victory at Tobruk but the men have rested and supplies are on the way. The Eighth Army, the message says, will be able to mount a strong counter-offensive in mid-September but not before, so now is the time to attack, providing petrol and ammo arrive as due. Date suggested 26 August, full moon. More evidence piles up. At the end of August, Montgomery wins the first defensive battle over Rommel at the Alam Halfa ridge, or rather, Rommel abandons the battle because, thanks to Ultra, and more especially to Mediterranean Naval Enigma now continually broken, the Allies have destroyed all the German ships sending supplies and fuel by the end of August. The Blitz too has ceased and the British and Americans are now bombing Germany non-stop. The Russians are holding the German advance, to everyone's surprise and perhaps shame, in the North where the Germans have been besieging Leningrad for months, and on the Central Front, and advancing slowly but relentlessly in the South, where Rostov and the Kerch peninsula fall. By September the Russians are defending Stalingrad street by street. There are more and more signs in the messages of German power shortage everywhere. At the end of October Montgomery pushes the Panzer Army back at Alamein. The Americans and English land in Morocco and Tunisia in November. On 31st of January '43 the Germans surrender at Stalingrad.

Some time around then Tess is picked off the Index, together with Jean Stelling and another girl, Leslie Tierney, Irish, ginger and witty, by Squadron-Leader Oscar Oeser, to start a new liaison section called 3L, by analogy with the air and military sections 3A and 3M. 3L occupies a cold room, all windows, added to the end of Hut 3, with no radiators, heated by a smelly oil-stove in the middle, a mindless risk to all the documents in

Hut 3. Oscar, unpopular but pleasant enough to the girls, is a psychologist from South Africa, square and small and dark with sleek black hair, a sleek black moustache, almond-shaped black eyes and a psycho's unsubtle hints of superior understanding. The new section also gets an army captain called George Craw-ford, a statistician from Hut 6, scruffy in battle-dress and no tie, but nobody cares about that here, many officers wear civvy slacks and sweaters, nobody goes round saluting anybody, not even the new CO of Hut 3, Group-Captain Jones, now secretaried by Jane Shields in a separate office.

Oscar's idea is to study the material day by day, straight from the German books, not real books but sheets of thin foolscap horizontally typed with many carbons and clipped together in brown paper, accumulating more and more tightly in the filing cabinets.

Why have the German books never been made available to historians? asks John the pedant, the ironic John..

Oh, do stop interrupting, John, memories are hard enough to get down.

Item by item as if each were an index-card.

Well each is in a way. And John the perk ordered itsybitsy not history. Presumably the famous Index has also been destroyed.

Also? The Index, okay, but the German books!

Jean Stelling, now Bradley, said Mrs Thatcher told historians all the German books had been burnt.

Impossible. A government can't destroy primary evidence. Might as well destroy parish registers. Without the typed-up German messages there's no proof, strictly speaking, in historians' terms, of any decoding.

Well, that's the situation. The official history and all the books about Ultra are written mostly from the translated teleprints sent to commanders in the field, merely cited in footnotes not textu-ally, and omitting the conventions used to indicate reliability, meaning degrees of corruption or uncorroborated detail, without call-signs or any other WTI, though WTI, even without any decoding, often told a precious story about troop movements. As with the transfer of units to Poland from Holland, for instance, before the German attack on Russia, Whitehall at first convinced

Poland must be a telemisprint for Holland. But perhaps the German books have been kept, and are not being deposited in the Public Record Office. Hardly matters in the long run.

And the run is getting longer and longer, soon every BP officer still alive will be dead. But human memories and anecdotes and personal desperate German messages not sent out to field commanders also make up history. The British Government is behaving like the KGB, and even the KGB has opened self-condemning old files to historians.

Quite. But the KGB and Communism crumbled, and the KGB sells access. If the old Houyhnhnm may be allowed to continue? The German books contain all the messages, key by key, frequency by frequency and day by day, with all the call-signs and WTI gen. Jean and Leslie and Tess have to analyse and grade the messages for George to calculate the changing daily value of every key and frequency and establish priority lists for the cryptographers and for the Fusion Room, now moved out of Hut 3 into a separate hut opposite.

What was the point, old lady?

Good question. With so many fields of action the volume intercepted has become huge, and the amount broken greater and greater. But to this day the old Houyhnhnm can't decide how useful 3L was, as opposed to being an ingenious invention of Oscar's to command a section. The German books aren't typed and distributed till the day after the material has been sent out, and the advisers on the Watch are already in constant touch with Hut 6 about the immediate value of any given key and the expenditure of bombe-time, same with the Fusion Room to the Y-stations about frequencies. But presumably 3L's results give back-up information, in a more statistical way, as well as continuous assessment of all the other, less operational admin and supply keys, in the Balkans, on the Russian Front. Certainly 3L is regularly visited by the big boffins from Hut 6, Josh Cooper, tall and shaggy and shy and mad-scientist-looking, Stuart Milner-Barry, a great chessman of more respectable appearance, or Gordon Welchman, mathematician and harpsichord-player. The following year Stuart will even take the girls to visit a new red block F where Colossus, the first giant computer, has replaced the old 'Heath Robinson' and lines the walls, manned by Wrens, as well as Hut 6, the inner sanctum, to show the Enigma machine, a large and clumsy typewriter. Stuart explains the mechanics, the three wheels inside, each day selected from eight possible wheels, each with all the letters of the alphabet all round, each placed every day in a different position and turning round for every letter typed, no letter being ever represented by the same letter, a useful elimination rule when working on cribs. This precious aid, Stuart will explain then, no longer exists for Tunny, or other 'Fish' links, the new non-morse machine for encoding and transmitting teleprinter impulses by radio, much harder to break than Enigma, less voluminous but carrying much higher-level messages, from Berlin and even Hitler to Army Group commanders, broken fairly regularly from January '43 on, thanks to Colossus.

At any rate, Tess is now reading the stuff in German, much more fun. Only a small proportion is translated and sent, so Tess also reads all kinds of human and humorous detail, like a furious complaint from some unit in Sidi Barani, desperate for fuel and spare parts but receiving a consignment of straw mats. And the girls now have access to intelligence reports from other sources, German secret agents' reports on Abwehr Enigma, POW interrogations and talk in bugged cells and tree-walks, Whitehall weekly summaries. Above all, Tess becomes liaison officer with the Fusion Room, now in the separate hut with steps because built on a highish hedge-bank, and puts up stars with pins and coloured strings all over the map on the wall, to see at a glance the frequencies used by each command to subordinate units. Soon Tess knows every frequency in the Luftwaffe, and all about callsigns and operator's chit-chat, and has constantly to visit the Fusion Room for checks, making several new friends.

One of these, a Major Wallace Farmery, comes from the North, reminding Tess of Plimsley, though handsomer. Wallace explains everything, and like Plimsley calls Tess highbrow, in the beer-hut, about popular music. But what about Cole Porter, or Duke Ellington, or Gershwin, or Irving Berlin, or Glenn Miller?

No. Tess looks blank. But Cole Porter wrote *Begin the Beguine*, Glenn Miller wrote *In the Mood*, and others wrote all the songs everyone's been singing and dancing to in the big brick new dance-hall just outside the gates. Tess had no idea these songs had composers, with names, and feels like Monsieur Jourdain discovering prose.

In the Fusion Room there is also a real composer in the bud, Ian Crane, wholly unlike Tess's idea of a composer. Tall and straight and twenty-three, Ian seems subsumed in a captain's uniform, with khaki hair, bulging khaki eyes and a face as pale as a khaki shirt. Ian doesn't walk, but marches. Marches along one morning and sees Tess in Waaf officer's greatcoat sitting on a dustbin outside the Hut 3 side-entrance opposite the new Fusion Room, reading a book to the last minute before going in. Like the mad hatter with the bicycle book, Ian is charmed.

Soon the charm becomes a routine, lunch or dinner in the canteen, according to the shift. Ian wants to become a composer, went to the Royal School of Music, takes Tess to see *Mrs Miniver, Cavalcade* and such, and talks about socialism.

Everyone moves out of the exiguous huts to a vast red brick building called Block D, a long series of cross-shapes, a wide corridor with right-angled narrower corridors and offices on either side. The Fusion Room is in Block G, behind. 3L now has three rooms, the largest for the girls. Ian visits often, or marches past on the way to the Watch whistling Mozart by way of secret message over the air. Ian is now WT adviser on the Watch, an innovation long due, as was the presence of a naval adviser soon after Tess's arrival. Tess, after being ASO then SO, has just been promoted to Flight Officer, or captain, with two full stripes on the wrist. But Tess has long ceased to care about stripes and badges.

The tide has turned, as Churchill and everyone says. Since Stalingrad the Russians are not just holding but bulging the German line back over that vast, more and more denuded front, less and less productive of important Enigma, but now luckily full of Fish. Since Alamein Montgomery is pursuing Rommel westwards across the Libyan desert, each time hesitating too long despite repeated Ultra evidence of Rommel's weakness, and each time letting the Panzer Army escape. This causes an explosion of fury in Hut 3, but will be the pattern all the way to Tunis, although

116

at Medenine in February Montgomery does mass troops at the precise point where Rommel had announced, a week earlier on Ultra, an about-turn to attack the 8th Army, and wins a total victory – Rommel leaves Africa. Hut 3 calms down. But in Tunisia the flow of army Enigma has dropped drastically since Christmas 1942 as the front moves North, the Germans having had time to build military landlines. The U-Boot war in the Atlantic has at last turned in favour of the Allies, largely thanks to Atlantic Naval Enigma more regularly broken now, especially the previously unreadable Shark. At least in cold statistics. For the British have lost vast quantities of what is horribly called tonnage, including Roland Rice-Jones. Mummy sees the announcement in *The Times* and instructs Tess to write, and Lady Rice-Jones sends a form to contribute to a memorial. Tess is piqued at this request for money from rich people and doesn't reply.

The Americans are now all over England, in olive-green, with Camel cigarettes and nylons and hard drinking, and there's even a small contingent in Hut 3, as Block D continues to be called. Tess and Jean were at first detailed to explain things to the advance CO, a Colonel Jon J. Timson, at a wide table in the big new Air Index room. But the Colonel seems to know a good deal already, and Tess, though proud to be doing any explaining at all to a senior officer, soon lets the colonel examine the cards alone. That's after all the way Tess learnt and the way the Colonel clearly prefers. The US section arrives and is lodged opposite 3L, soon becoming very friendly and dropping in with funny accents for coffee and lunching together after a drink in the beer-hut. Today the British, of whatever class, have the funny accent, the quaint archaic accent.

One evening shift, back from the canteen, Ian follows Tess into the empty office and becomes gauche in the public school manner Tess has come to know from Janet's brother Peter, now in the RAF and once seen on leave. Ian stutters out some phrase about supposing Tess knows, well, Ian is in love.

Yes.

This is followed by a chaste kiss, captain to captain. In soldier-miming-film position.

The next day that yes to a specific question has been silently

117

metamorphosed by Ian into a much bigger yes to an unmade proposal. As if Ian had taken Tess's arm to cross a street as code for asking Tess's hand and wanting Tess's all. Ian's father is rung. An advertisement is put in *The Times*. Tess is in an impasse of impotence oddly turned to impetus. A striangulation. At an awkward lunch in the canteen Ian is introduced to mummy, quietly pleased and shy, impressed by Ian's good manners and obvious devotion. Ian does all the talking. An engagement can always be broken, Tess silently reflects. Tess has noticed how partners are constantly changing at BP, couples having coffee together on the lawn, or skating together on the lake, according to the seasons, then not.

Ian is of course full of admiration for Tess's studies. All Tess's mentors seem charmed by the image given of a serious girl hungry for knowledge, yet swiftly do everything to quench that hunger and possess Tess's time, replacing the knowledge sought with other knowledge, the knowledge of the mentor, no doubt also needed but not necessarily then. For hunger has a secret time-table.

Instead of studying, bicycle rides again or the flicks, or listening to Tess's records. Any request to spend an evening alone is met with accusations of not loving, a blackmail unknown to Tess and unfaced, since Tess doesn't know love. Leaves are now spent with Ian's friends in Kent, via dinner in London with Ian's father, a benign barrister in black and pinstripe, at the University Club. A widower, for Ian's mother, an actress and writer, committed suicide, leaving a memory of brilliance and fame Tess has never heard of. The mother's friend Isobel, a tiny ginger lady with horsy teeth living with a ginger son Robin so far wangled out of any national service, becomes the second home. Robin talks of cars, and of plastics as the material of the future. Plastics? Plasticine? Isobel gives Tess two flat rolls of prewar material from Ian's mother, a splendid red and gold brocade and a royal blue taffeta in barely visible narrow stripes, of slightly paler blue. Sometimes a night is chastely spent in London, in service rooms at Hans Place, to take in a prom at the Albert Hall, now the old Queen's Hall is bombed out, or a play, Gielgud in *Hamlet*, open-shirted and over-acting, silly pansy, says Ian, whatever that means. All pleasant enough, but Tess's entire way of life, with Janet and Jock for leaves, is unquestioningly annulled.

And Ian teaches Tess, at last, the Facts of Life, the one fact so incredibly unknown, despite Ovid. Ian is as appalled by Tess's ignorance, but also pleased and jocular, as Tess is appalled both by the book Ian buys and by having reached twenty without knowing the Fact. And Tess soon learns outside the book, for Ian goes in for heavy all-but petting, virginity being hypocritically respected then, and Tess handles a man's penis in erection for the first time, feeling no desire but going through the taught motions to please. Tess still can't imagine this thing penetrating a tiny hole, isn't even aware of having a tiny hole. But Ian takes Tess to a gynaecologist in Harley Street for advice on female contraception, mysteriously called Dutch cap, and after examination the doctor declares the hymen to be so tough Tess'd scream the place down or else never consummate (due to the early heel-habit?). Tess is relieved. Fancy the body being a fortress against invasion! But the doctor suggests a surgical removal. Ian acquiesces. Sicily falls in August.

Unbelievable, mutters John[1] to John[1].

Meaning Sicily? And this despite the failure of the Allies to use the intelligence sent and follow on fast as some 60,000 Germans and 70,000 Italians escape to the mainland in mid-August, much to the amused scorn of German commanders including Kesselring as gleefully expressed in messages from Calabria.

But the Facts of Life at last learnt leave Tess indifferent as a flat iron. Not disgusted, as mummy was, just distastefully resigned. And soon Ian's horizons are revealed as irritatingly limited to dirty limericks and ready-made jokes, irritating not because dirty but because ready-made and repeated, chortled noisily with intermittent squeaks. Here's a good one, Ian says in the beer-hut: What's the definition of a titbit?... A Mosquito-raid on Brest. Chortle. Oh hello, Geoffrey, repeat, over. Ian seems to have no natural wit, and Tess hasn't yet learnt the wifely duty of enduring the husband's public as well as private performance.

In Kent, during a walk, Tess breaks off the engagement. Huge distress, threats of suicide, with the mother's death hidden inside the threat. Is such power possible? Tess is frightened. Tiny toothy

Isobel finds Tess crying. There there etc, Ian is very upset. So the engagement is on. Broken again later with a run-to-mother. Oh darling such a pity. Such a fine young man. All the odder since Ian as declared atheist has freed Tess from any remnants of school or Broughton Hall veneer back into godless childhood. But darling, at least Ian will be faithful. So the engagement is on again. Why did women do this?

In January 1944 Tess gives a twenty-first birthday party in the Park Hotel for everyone not on evening shift. Barrels of beer, sandwiches, singing and dancing. A happy time is had by all including Tess in huge self-convince. There's a surprise landing in Anzio. The Russians break the siege of Leningrad. The wedding is planned for April.

Tess discovers cowardice about breaking when all arrangements are made and presents received and invitations sent out. The Russians invade the Crimea. The wedding takes place in Kensington. Jock gives Tess away. Jock and Janet, mummy, Vanna and André, Joanne about to leave for Naples, Ian's father, Isobel and Robin represent the two very incomplete families, the other guests are all BP. The Waaf messengers, for some reason under Tess's mythical command, form a guard of honour. Tess wears pale turquoise, clashing with Jock's blue-grey and Ian's khaki. Mad! screams Joanne at the reception, in Wren officer's uniform, how unlucky to get married in green! That's Joanne's only good wish, and Tess rather agrees.

The honeymoon is spent in the Scillies, well-named, and at last the marriage is consummated, but so badly Tess finds little joy. For despite the sexy jokes, Ian knows little more than Tess does, and rouses by furiously agitating the minuscule clitoris till Tess comes, Ian mistaking this for readiness and then penetrating, to swollen resistance and pain. This mechanical technique will continue throughout the marriage, nor does Tess decode as ignorance, assuming this is sex, and awful as mummy somehow implied. What Tess does decode at once, but for many other reasons, is the marriage as a mistake. Rommel takes charge in Europe against the long expected Second Front, where, because of landlines, Enigma has been non-existent, but replaced, haphazardly, by the scarcer but much more important Fish. With the fighting, and the destruction of landlines, Enigma bursts out again, though gapfully at first, hence the failure to take Caen at once – soon the volume rises again. Work becomes hectic.

A bathless cottage (but there's a bath-hut at BP) in Stewkley, the longest village in England with a pretty Norman church. Tess learns to cook British, reading wartime recipes, how to make the one piece of meat or one rasher of bacon or the one egg a week go further with wartime sausages, offal, potatoes, powdered egg. Rome falls to the Allies. The Second Front begins at last, in Normandy, the Germans having mostly but not entirely expected Calais. Work is intense, exciting, exhausting. There's an upright piano Ian plays, and to Tess's astonishment is not much further than Tess was at school, staying with the easier Mozart sonatas. Tess had assumed composers master at least one instrument, but apparently not, the music must all come out of composer's heads. What comes out of Ian's head is a solitary chord, played often, part of a future symphony. Tess admires enthusiastically but thinks of Jimmy Durante's *The Lost Chord*. And quite soon comes the announcement, honest enough: Ian would rather not be a composer at all than a second-rate composer. Tess will long remember those brave words in future struggles to write. Ian is going to take up law. Law! Gone are the last wisps of garret-starving with a musician.

The doodlebugs begin, Hitler's secret weapon long monitored by Hut 3 and considerably reduced by raids on Peenemunde, but frightening all the same, with that nerve-jerking silence after the rumble, meaning now, near. But most fall further South than Buckinghamshire. The Italian campaign is slowed down by diversion of Allied forces to France, unexpected German resistance and bad use of intelligence. Ian sends for big books on Roman Law and the Law of Tort, and a nutshell series including *The Carriage of Goods by Sea in a Nutshell*, chortle. The jokes become legal jokes, playing on set phrases, breaking and entry and aggravated buggery, conduct calculated to cause a breach of promise (Tess smiles), loitering with intent to feel. But perhaps the old lady has invented these, the real jokes forgotten. Ian oddly makes Tess read A.P. Herbert's funny books on law, including *Holy Deadlock* on the absurdities and difficulties of divorce.

Montgomery gets stuck in the Falaise pocket, but the Allies eventually struggle on. Paris falls (is liberated) in August. Rommel is killed in a car accident but in fact suicided after the failed Staufenberg attempt on Hitler's life in July. The Russians now have Rumanian oil, at least the little left after American bombing. The Russians stop a few miles from Warsaw, letting the Germans raze the city. Hut 3 warns Montgomery of two German Panzer divisions near Arnhem, in vain.

The Allies reach the Rhine, at least here and there, in Holland and down in Strasbourg, even if the Atlantic coast still has German pockets. German messages are getting more and more desperate. Ian gets pneumonia and is taken to hospital in Luton, where Tess hitches down the Great North Road to visit. But seizes the occasion to satisfy curiosity and provoke an affair with the only too willing Colonel Jon J. Timson, sixteen years older at thirty-seven, married with two young daughters, also a lawyer, playing the piano much better, a sort of superior replica of Ian but looking like Gary Cooper. Tess half hopes this will give produce the courage to break.

But soon Tess is also ill, can't visit Ian, is visited in Sick Bay by Jon J. explaining the American election of Roosevelt for an unprecedented fourth term, don't change horses in mid-stream as slogan, and Tess laughs, for Tess has a urinary infection and has to give mid-stream urine samples. But Jon J. understands the laugh as for changing men. Tess hasn't had this trouble since childhood and wonders if sex is the cause. At least there are sulphonomides now, no wet sheets to bring the fever down, and soon Tess is out.

The war drags on, to general discouragement after the wave of hope brought by the Second Front, when everyone thought the war would be over in a few weeks. During November and early December an unheard of 6th Panzer Army appears in the messages, with Volskwagen cars. WT indication piles up of a counter-offensive in the Ardennes, but so fragmentary, because of radio-silence with only minimal checking contacts, nobody believes the evidence. Mere boys, says Whitehall, and Volkswagen cars. Yet the Allied Front, thanks to Eisenhauer, is thinly strung all the way down to Alsace, and the Germans did use the Ardennes to pierce through in 1940. The idea could well be to split the Allies, the British in the North from the Americans further South, and cause another Dunkirk. In mid-December the Germans attack, with massive Tiger tanks, pushing the Americans back, mostly young recruits just arrived, in filthy freezing weather. Surrenders galore, the SS executing prisoners, and 9,000 needlessly dead. The Battle of the Bulge.

When Ian returns Tess tells. Ian goes into shock. But is soon magnanimous alas, convinced all will blow over, behaves like an English gentleman, has a serious talk and shakes hands with Jon J., much to Jon J.'s amusement. All does not blow over. Not for the sex, swift and wiggly and comeless for Tess, but for the new, astonishing experience of desire, opening up without pain, and the secret walks and talks about American and British law, more mysteriously alive than anything Ian tells. For Tess may well later complain of quenching by mentors, but has also learnt to use people as founts of knowledge, mentowers as mentors.

Ian and Tess spend a first Christmas Eve together, miserably, on duty. In January the Americans roll back the Ardennes offensive. Tess begins to wonder whether the Allies are not winning this war by sheer fluke and American plenty. The advancing armies discover the first death-camps, known to exist but not in such full horror. Nothing of this was ever hinted at in all those operational orders and sitreps. Tess decides Hailey must be a Jewish name, wants passionately to be a Jew. The Allies are closing in on Berlin and bomb Dresden off the map, unnecessarily since there are no military targets around and Hut 3 says so. South American states as well as Turkey, Lebanon, Syria, Egypt, Saudi Arabia and Finland belatedly declare war on Germany. In March the Big Three carve up Europe at Yalta, moving the very frontiers Britain had guaranteed and gone to war for and arranging for Allied armies to stop short of Berlin, Vienna and Prague. Tess wonders what generals and politicans are for. Roosevelt dies, little Truman takes over.

The affair does at last give Tess the courage to break for good. Drama etc. Ian goes off on compassionate leave. Jon J. and Tess can now enjoy freely. The Russians reach Berlin as arranged, Hitler has committed suicide in a bunker, Mussolini has already been shot by partisans and hung by the heels, the Russians reach Vienna. Jon J. has been nominated to the War Crime Tribunal and flies to Washington for consultation. (Why are the equally criminal Russians being allowed to sit in judgment on Nazi war crimes? Tess had asked.) Jon J. promises to try for a divorce. Tess is left alone, still in touch via Group Captain Jones. But the sprint has slackened, quite suddenly. Tess continues to play the bereft, but is secretly glad to be rid of both men.

At last the war in Europe is over. Jon J. is back and meets Tess on the evening of VE-Day, in St James's Park, on the bridge, among all the celebrating crowds and the fireworks. Tess and Jon J. walk away and sit on the grass. No divorce. Tess is relieved, has no longing to abandon future studies once again and live in New York. A much easier break than with Ian. This is a bit like daddy's death. But not wholly, for now Tess can say: alone at last, the war is over, real life begins.

10. FILE: VICTRICKS

Enigma traffic is silent now, as silent as memory will be for nearly thirty years, and still is for great gaps unreleased or burnt, lost for ever. Bletchley Park is half-empty, people have scattered. Oscar and other IOs left weeks ago, accompanying advance troops to capture German documents and gear and men for interrogation. Jim Hardy, now a Wing-Commander, is at the Air Ministry, mummy is cooking for a Catholic lay-community of professional women in Chelsea. After VE-Day Tess returns to the empty cottage and to Hut 3-Block D, where a much reduced staff is working from CX/MSS and cards on what is to become the official history, never released.

Just as well, says John the pedant, Tess's bit being probably gibberish by an untrained girl.

And Tess votes for the first time, accompanying Janet after election-day to an Old Girls' gathering at SSC, evacuated to Taplow. But Tess has long evacuated SSC, has no intercept with the few girls remembered, some married with children, all very jolly, very society. The results are being broadcast during the bun-tea, to general groans: a Labour landslide. Then one of the girls sees Tess's face, and Janet's, both veeish for victory. Traitors! Ooh! And laughter.

The lights go up all over England, the black-out curtains vanish. In August the first atom-bomb is dropped on Japan, then the second, to the solemn horror guiltily tinged with relief of all those around Tess, contrary to the triumphantly gleeful Schadenfreude of the press. The war just fought seems suddenly quaint, archaic.

Then Jim Hardy calls Tess from the Air Ministry, to work at the British Bombing Survey Unit, BBSU, much less exciting or secret, but this does mean London, the end of Bletchley, the end of supposedly official history. Tess packs the few belongings in the cottage, leaving the rest and the wedding presents, the silver ramekin dishes, the toast rack etc, to Ian, and finds an attic room in the Cromwell Road, up many stairs, with a sloping window full of sky.

The work is dull but Tess meets many people. One Wing-Commander is flying to Hanover via Brussels, and offers Tess a lift, just for the lark. Brussels! Oncle Francis and Tante Mathilde are back there from Geneva, and Tess finds unfamiliar family feelings, in fact mere curiosity.

A car collects Tess and drives to Hounslow. The plane seems to be a Mosquito, adapted for transport. The Wing-Commander and navigator are in front, there's only one passenger seat in the khaki fuselage and no loo, just a big tube at the back like a gas mask's corrugated elephant-trunk sticking out of the floor on a hook. Over the channel the air-baptism becomes a torture, for Tess is bursting, can't even look out of the window, and at last gets up to use the tube, back turned to the pilots and greatcoat open as screen. But Tess has nothing to aim with (as Freud keeps insisting, says John the perk), and with the shaking of the aircraft pees all over the khaki metal floor, as in Chiswick over the pink carpet. The officers gallantly pretend not to notice when the plane lands in Evere, from where mummy took off when daddy died, and drive Tess in a jeep to l'avenue de l'Opale nearby. Twelve-thirty. Tess is given two hours.

There' a lot of peeing in this remake, says John the psycho.

Not as much as in the original. Like all those lost thoughts John the perk didn't want in.

Up in the lift, the coffin for grandpère's coffin, to the fifth floor. The familiar bell-code, meaningless probably. The door is opened by a tubby little woman, much shorter than Tess and almost unrecognizable as Tante Mathilde – how can anyone change so in seven years? – and Oncle Francis behind, unaltered apart from grey hair, both astonished at this Waaf officer last seen as a girl of fifteen.

The bedroom on the right of the hall, with the knobbled glass panes in grey-blue frames, where Tess played with Jean-Luc, seems tiny. Talk over lunch is chiefly about Geneva and the Red

Cross and Oncle Francis now trying to revive the Voyages Blair, and dramatic versions of life in Geneva, life in Brussels before, when grandpère monopolized the drawing-room every evening to listen to Radio Moscow, no social life possible, Tante Mathilde was sidérée! Dieu merci! grandpère never lived to see the Hitler-Stalin pact! Dieu merci, tout est fini etc. There are no questions about Tess.

After lunch Tante Mathilde takes Tess up in the lift to the attic to see the toys and books in a trunk. And there are the dolls Sylviane et Marianne in brown curls and blue velvet and rabbit fur, and all the books. But not Pooh Bear. Pooh Bear accompanied Tess to Folkestone and was packed away for the duration. Tess says give away the lot. Not till many decades later, as an old lady at the age of reminiscence, will there come a pinch of regret for that lordly gesture, not over the dolls but over the books, *Sans famille, Les petites filles modèles, Le général Dourakine, Pauvre Blaise* and the rest (was Tess's morality derived from la Comtesse de Ségur?), the school histories about Berthe au Grand Pied and Godefroy de Bouillon and Charlequint, Flemish exercises, the French grammar, so closely printed compared to those children have today, laying out all the conjugations and the rules about plurals of mots composés and l'accord du participe passé, learnt by heart every day, therefore still known. And the anthology, with a poem never found since: *Si la Garonne avait voulu*, the river would have gone to all sorts of places, named and described, would have invaded Spain. *Mais la Garonne n'a pas voulu*, and went to Toulouse. Tess felt like la Garonne, and la Garonne now seems to summarize the old lady's life. But nostalgia, useless at all times, seems only to come with age. Hanover and back is unremembered.

Tess works hard at the Ministry, on documents and statistics, but is soon sent to Germany, the American Zone, together with a stunning blond Waaf officer called Barbara, also from Bletchley. The plane to Frankfurt is a long American Dakota with facing khaki metal seats along the curved khaki fuselage walls, very unlike the solitary looless seat. And there Tess does look out of the window, enchanted with the paintbrush fields, for the Dakota flies much higher.

The old Houyhnhnm has no memory of Tess's work in Frankfurt, only of the fun, mildly marred by a squeamishness about occupation, for Tess is constantly upset by the way the driver hoots Germans off the ruined streets and by all Allied staff being billeted in the few unruined blocks of flats, some liberating books and objects, but also by the obsequiousness of the German waiters in the huge officers' mess on the ground floor of the still standing IG Farben building. Here Tess tries out the slow jump-in lifts, to test mummy's unimaginable description of the lifts at the ILO in Geneva. The description was true.

All fraternization is strictly forbidden, but illegal night expeditions are organized to a man in a suburb making real leather bags and wallets, paid for with cigarette cartons from the PX. The Americans have plenty of everything, the Germans are starving and scrambling. Perhaps all that daily reading of the war from the other side, with all those innumerable little human touches unnecessary to Whitehall, has made Tess soft. Five years later, in the early fifties, when travelling all over poverty-stricken Spain with Janek, long before the arrival of mass tourism, Tess will feel the same dismay at the beggar children, señorita, una pesetina, por favor, tengo hambre, señorita. For Janek and Tess are also poor, if not as poor as that, saving every penny for these trips and travelling rough, very rough, often with the chickens and pigs, and Tess is thrown by the role of the then rare rich tourist, as now thrown by the role of conquering occupier. Today the beggars are in Paris, London, New York.

Warlords' wars affect so many unwarlike. How much mere chance put Tess on the winning side? If George Blair (Vanderbilt) had not been sent to Geneva as a boy, but stayed with the Bodenhausens and married a German minor aristocrat, the whole family would have been German. And with that ignorance and naivety and urge to meld, wouldn't Tess also have belonged to the Bund der Deutsche Mädel and later done warwork? But then, Tess would not have been Tess. As John the perk would say, the ifs of history are unlived, unuttered narratives. If mummy had married the Californian painter – but then Tess would not have been Tess. As Tess, there was the refused raised arm and the mumbled To Hell Hitler in Ulm, but the unprotesting bewilderment at Gerd's lessons about the Führer.

Barbara has no such squandered qualms, chatting happily in German with members of the bands playing *A Sennimennal Journey* and the rest in scattered castles. Barbara is squired by two American officers, one a Polish Prince Sapieha, the other a conductor and both in love, strung along amiably and without drama. The four jeep together all over the forests of Hessen, and visit 'Dustbin', a big castle for top Nazi prisoners, and scrounge a flight to Berlin, billeted in a smart villa in Charlottenburg, the American Zone relatively unbombed, spared as if in anticipation. Tess is astonished to peer at horse-drawn military vehicles among the ruins of the forbidden area beyond the Brandenburg Gate. But then, in retrospect, John the pedant insists, all wars, however modern-seeming at the time, have always been weird mixtures of the primitive and hitec. So does peace for that matter, why are streets still drilled open to get at the pipes and cables, why not a kind of zip-opener? Return by truck through the forests of the Russian Zone, not allowed to stray an inch off the Autobahn till the control at Helmstedt in the British Zone. A herd of cows ambles across an overhead bridge. So that's an Autobahn. Tess is shattered by shattered Kassel, where hardly a house is standing. All rubble, far worse than London or Liverpool. But also in Essen, Köln, Düsseldorf and others, says Barbara, not to mention Dresden in the Russian zone, and the towns of Northern France, bombed by the Allies to prevent German reinforcements, Brest, Caen, Rouen, and those of Eastern France demolished by retreating Germans. Ground fighting incidentally leaves towns completely rased, air-bombing leaves walls standing. No, Tess didn't know. Military transport is used for private pleasure. Everyone sleeps with everyone. But Tess's few attempts, for mere reassurance, are still nil and ill-enjoyed. What's all the fuss about?

In an ex-dancehall turned military mess in Hoechst, near Frankfurt, the group walks in, and Tess notices a scuffle on the right. The scuffle is Ian, walking out precipitately with a pretty ATS officer. So the suicide threat wore off. Good.

Tess is waiting in the air-hut with other officers flying back to London. Names are called out. Flight Officer Crane. In the aircraft, a handsome Flight Lieutenant sits next to Tess on the long side-bench and addresses Tess as Ian's ex-wife. And very pretty too, Ian is a fool. And so on. A pick-up and no mistake. Tess sighs. Name of Sean. But that evening the two go out to a night-club and dance in aroused rhythms, then climb to the attic room and make love on the single bed. Tess's first experience of pleasure, beyond the pain. Untaught, ill-initiated, Tess at twenty-two at last begins to understand. So that's what sex is all about. Not revulsion, not pain, not romantic infatuation by way of escape, not silly experiments, not even love, just fun, laughter and stimulus, neither having a care for the future.

One morning there's a knock on the door. Tess is naked in bed with Sean and slips on a shabby Japanese kimono from the thirties, passed on by mummy. The landlady? No, Jon J. is standing there, slightly puffed from the stairs, a general now, but still like Gary Cooper. Must have got the address from Jim. Tess holds the door closed behind and the kimono closed in front.

Go away.

But honey –

What right –

Tess plays the virtuous victim of abandonment, to stop Jon J. coming in.

Look. Presents. Perfume. Nylons.

Please Jon, please go away.

Jon J. turns, crumpled, and slowly walks down the stairs.

My, says Sean when Tess explains. Married to one man, in love with another and making love to a third. Not at all the inno-cent little thing married too young for one year.

But Tess is not in love with another. Or with the third. Nor does Tess mention the here-and-there experiments in Germany, the one-night or one-minute stands causing Tess to wonder why men make such a thing of sex though so incompetent, that being, Tess now reflects, the reason.

The affair goes on, happily, when Sean is in London, or in Germany. For Tess is sent to Frankfurt again. This time the task is to visit a prisoners' camp North of Munich and interrogate one Schleuermann, head of all the bomb damage statistics. BBSU wants to know where these are. When Tess gets clearance from American Intelligence in the IG Farben building the officer says

130

Schleuermann? Schleuermann is wanted here. In Dustbin Castle. Bring the man back.

What! Escort a prisoner?

Sure. The regulations say an officer-and-a-man. The driver's a man, that'll fit the tag.

Talking of castles, Tess asks the officer whether US Intelligence has any information about the German owners of the small Schloss near Ulm, vague prewar friends, Tess adds. The officer checks. Sure. Under house-arrest as Nazis.

So off Tess goes in a fifteen hundredweight truck, slowly along the snowed-up, iced-up Autobahn, into Franconia and Bavaria. There are just two seats in front, so presumably Tess will have to guard the prisoner in the truck part on the way back. This is mad. The truck drives via Nüremberg and has to stop overnight, Tess in an officers' mess, the driver in another. Tess thinks, well, Jon J. is here in Nüremberg, about to start on the wartrials. Would a surprise visit –? But thinks better, best, no, and eats alone in the officer's mess. After dinner, Tess walks up and down in the snow, listening to a friendly German waiter intent on proving how the Allies made a big mistake not joining Hitler against the Communists. The Russians have been called gallant Russian allies since the German attack, never Communists. Even the Russian Zone is called Russian, not Soviet, though Soviet Union will be imposed for forty-five years before becoming ex and then Russia again. So Tess is surprised, but says vielleicht and doch, or at most how impossible for the Allies to switch sides just because Hitler invaded Russia. But the German waiter doesn't mean that, agrees with that, the German waiter means earlier. But earlier Hitler was an ally of Stalin. Ja natürlich, but the German waiter means, Tess doesn't know, but the meaning is spoken with the passionate conviction of regret. Perhaps the German waiter merely wants to show Tess how some Germans were on the Allied side all along.

At the camp, North of Munich (could this have been Dachau provisionally readapted, now visitable as Dachau? Surely not, but impossible to find out today), a dismal collection of low huts behind barbed wire, Tess produces the orders. After a long wait, a little man is shown into the guardroom, wearing pyjamas under an overcoat and thick muffler. Schleuermann is ill. Can't travel. Has a doctor's certificate.

Tess consults the driver. Can the truck get back in one day, in this weather, by the Southern route?

No ma'am. Ever so crowded. Took the Neuenberg road cos there's less traffic.

So what would happen overnight?

Well ma'am, the prisoner'd 'ave to be clapped in jug. Ma'am.

But the man's got pneumonia. The responsibility's too great.

That's right ma'am.

So Tess questions Schleuermann, at least to get the British part of the task done. And the upshot is, all the documents about bomb-damage are in Jena. Jena is in the Russian Zone.

Mission failed. The whole trip for nothing. So ends the adventure as officer and man, Tess says to the driver back in the truck. The driver clearly thinks Tess a rum young lady.

Two years ago the old lady made a Sennimennal Journey back to wartime scenes. First to Bletchley, with Jean Stelling.

But that recontact started earlier, puts in John the pedant, remember? A letter from Jean, look, dated 1983, after thirty-eight years of silence since the end of Bletchley Park, enclosing that cutting from *The Times* about Ian's sudden death at sixty-three.

Ah yes. Says Ian was a judge, leaving a wife and two children. Jean had seen Ian only a week before, to find out more about MI8. Because Jean is working on Ultra, or rather, then, on a German spy in Egypt called Almassy, and is full of that. Seems Jean is as fixated on warwork as any old general. Says how proud Ian was of Tess.

And the visit, in Kensington.

Tess receiving a narcissistic shock when a sturdy old battle-axe opens the door. But then, Jean was eight years older, the old Houyhnhnm still has that to come.

Nonsense, old lady, Jean probably has the same shock.

Touchée. Such a relief, Jean says, when Freddy Winterbotham was first allowed to break the silence in '73, with *The Ultra Secret*.

Jean seems to use first names for all the invisible high-ups, even Winston, says John the pedant.

At last Jean could talk! Mummy was a spy! Granny was a spy! So funny after years of being a mere housewife.

Hence the replunging.

How strange. If Tess had remained married to Ian, the old Houyhnhnm would now be a widow .Would have been a lawyer's wife in London, with the children Janek though so virile couldn't give, and no books written.

Children are rarely a loyal comfort in old age, the old parents just a duty.

And if Tess had married Jon J., a lawyer's wife in New York, but not a widow. For Jon J. is still alive, well over eighty, has kept in touch all these years on and off, did divorce after all, much later, to marry a charming young lawyer and have two more children, and comes to Provence, nearby, every summer. But then, nearly all the old lady's lovers flirts and friends have remained in touch or recontacted later. That's peculiarly comforting. Even Janet and Jock, both now dead.

Oh, the ifs of history, says John. If daddy hadn't known the Smiths Tess and Joanne would never have gone to that semi-posh school.

And would have had a horrible accent!

But the Sennimennal Journey?

Yes. On another visit to Jean Bradley née Stelling, at the end of a winter stay in London. Jean says there's a Bletchley Park Archaeological Society wanting to buy the place up from British Telecom and create an Ultra Museum. The old Houyhnhnm feels like a shard of ancient pottery. The president has invited the two old ladies down, to interview on video.

So Jean and the old lady travel down to Bletchley, on a modern and much faster train, open-plan not corridorless carriages, leaving from the brightly airported Euston Station. Jean is now working on Yugoslavia for a BBC programme and talks of that all the way down, past the familiar though fewer stops, Watford Junction, Hemel Hempstead, Dunstable, Leighton Buzzard, how Fitzroy Maclean misled Churchill about the Serb Mihailovic in favour of the Croat and Communist Tito, changing the course of history. Jean is pro-Serb, projecting all that complex guerrilla warfare Tess used to pin up on the map, onto the present even more horrendous conflict. Jean is also convinced the reports written every week by the girls for Oscar went straight to Winston, on Winston's orders, and this can't be true. Oscar died many years ago so can't be checked. The old lady wonders if Tess megaloed too – no, says John – but lets Jean talk, can hardly do otherwise, for Jean is endearingly obsessed and muddled, accumulating more and more details into a computer for a mythical book.

A car is waiting at the station, and Bletchley is unrecognizable, with a huge roundabout near the railway bridge making the Park Hotel now only accessible from behind. The car drives in freely, without a pass, to the Main Building, long and red and white and unchanged but insistently called The Mansion by the squat little chairman inside. The shabby hall and offices are now carpeted and open-planned and very grand. There is a small film-crew, and Mr and Mrs Anthony Sale, much more congenial and soon clung to by the old ladies. Anthony Sale, from the Science Museum, is trying to reconstruct Colossus. Presumably, the old lady asks, computers can now devise truly unbreakable codes? Answer: Well, any computer-devised code is in theory breakable by another computer. The only unbreakable code is much more primitive, on a sheet of paper changed for every message, all the sheets possessed at both ends. Far too cumbersome of course, but perhaps now, with computers able to produce the equivalent code for each message, well, why not? Mr Sale naturally has no idea of what goes on at the present-day GCHQ near Cheltenham.

The beer-hut has become a car-park, the grey cement tennis court is cracked, weedy and bedraggled. Hut 6 is unchanged in the dirty white clapboard, though now greenish, but Hut 3 has been dressed in boarding painted bright ochre. The squat little chairman has the keys. The long corridor is dilapidated, the loo filthy, the small offices all empty, the Watch in the angle is rid of the gallant round table and just has chairs piled up in a corner. The hatches are blocked up. All strikingly dead.

Beyond the angle, another corridor with small rooms on either side. Jean can't understand why the Index Room on the right is so small. The old Houyhnhnm's memory, however faulty on some things, is relentlessly topological and sees at once how the long

134

wide room has been divided up by a new corridor and offices. But to the left nothing has changed, the first Fusion Room, the Map Room, and, at the very end, the first 3L. Despite the effort at mental reconstruction, everything seems small. And fifty years decrepit.

Outside the side-entrance there is still a dustbin, perhaps the same Tess sat on, opposite the second Fusion Room or MI8 Hut with now ruined steps to the elevated ruined door. And beyond the huts, looking for redbrick Block D, the old lady sees only low dirty cream buildings.

But those are in fact Block D – and E and G behind – repainted, much lower than remembered. The squat little chairman unlocks the door of the main entrance. Inside, a brick wall blocks the long wide central corridor linking all the transverse sections, so the party has to go out again and enter by a side-door in the next transverse section, never used at the time. Here the neglect howls. There are dangerous holes in the floor and water every-where. The pipeline hatch to Hut 6 is blocked, but above, all along the corridor ceiling, the zoom-pipes for the messages, as in old-fashioned shops, are still there. The Air Index room is found, huge this time, and the Watch, and the little side-room where the Waafs received and distributed the messages to the Watch and the TPs to everyone. Tess visualizes the round table, the advisers' table and the hatch to the Duty Officer and beyond, the room of the teleprincesses. And, in the opposite corner near the Waafs' room, was the WTI adviser's table where Ian sat, or colleagues.

Across the wide corridor into the other transverse, right at the end, is 3L, with Oscar's and George's little rooms next door and the American room opposite. Dirty, empty, dreary pieces of past. Impossible to believe time there was so operational, so tense, so knowledgeably alive.

John the pedant reminds the old lady of the same disbelief felt on reading the six volumes of the official Ultra history, not dilapidated but glossy and expensive, yet so dead: how could anything so perpetually exciting be made so dull?

True. With hardly any names either. Bletchley Park through-out is GC & CS, specific nobs in Whitehall and in the field are called JIS, JPS, DDMI, CBME, CIU, VCAS and other such dehauntological names, oh with a glossary of course, but un-readable as story. To protect the bunglers probably. But is that history? If the Last Judgment is like that God must be desolated with boredom and further research into human hearts.

Well, yes, but at least the official history is accurate and detailed. Unlike the video made on that day, a blurred and amateurish mishmash of old stills already published elsewhere, of the Main Building (The Mansion), of the Huts, of the Wrens working the Bombe in total ignorance, of the old ladies made to walk over and over down the added corridor in the old Hut 3 reconstructing how things were, but the words cut, the interviews cut, both women captioned erroneously as decoders. The Bletchley Archaeological Society, demonstrating how falsely history is made, surely won't get much sponsoring for that.

The old ladies are taken to a luxury lunch at the Park Hotel, now an elegant lounge-pub with restaurant. Tess asks the waiter if there is still a room for parties at the top of the house, no, the top of the house is all rooms for waiters.

Driving back from England to Provence, the old lady makes a huge detour, now the Wall has crumbled, via Berlin and East Germany, through Belgium and Holland to Hanover and Helm-stedt, now a simple motorway gas-station but with the Iron Curtain control buildings still there. To see friends but also the ex-DDR before total absorption, a paradox of private Com-munist débrouillardise and inertia, the Western cousins will do things better and say so. And perhaps to find the office of the Abwehr, that inefficient German Intelligence Bureau, at 28 Tirpitz Ufer. Bernhard hunts on the map along the Schiffsfahrt-kanal, for the streets along the Spree are not called Ufer. But there is no Tirpitz Ufer, just as there is no Tirpitz, sunk by the British. Finally Bernhard buys a republished prewar map of Berlin and tracks down Tirpitz Ufer, now renamed Reichspietsch Ufer, and showing the emplacement of the Kriegsministerium or OKH, so familiar and even friendly from daily reading. The old lady drives there with Bernhard and Rima. No 28 is merely part of the huge fascist-style building, now housing the Social Security and there-fore open to the public. At the entrance, the space for the old plaque is still visible, the new plaque merely placed above. Inside the immense hall, silent and empty, with marble columns and a monumental stone staircase, same thing: the direction panels on the columns are placed above or below the visible traces of the old panels, merely taken down, leaving rough unmarbled rectangles. Ghosts of OKH.

There will be other ghosts in Saxony and Thüringen. Jena for one, black-tenemented or dark grey, where the old lady thinks, not of Napoleon's battle, nor of IENA as a Paris bridge or a frequent solution in French crosswords, nor of Hegel et al, but of poor little sick Schleuermann and the bomb-damage statistics needed by BBSU, presumably now lying uselessly in the ex-KGB.

Another bladder infection, another stay in the military Sick Bay of a London hospital. In the ward is a middle-aged lady Tess recognizes as Section Officer Stevenson, the WAAF CO at Thornaby-on-Tees. Tess goes over to talk, but notices the tunic on the chair, with still only one ring on the sleeve. SO Stevenson has noticed Tess's too, with two stripes, and is cool. And Tess feels oddly ashamed, not proud, to have reached captain's rank while the CO over twice as old has spent the whole war without promotion.

In January 1946 Tess is demobbed, at just twenty-three. And having saved assiduously on that captain's pay with low expenses in Bletchley, decides to use those £500, a small fortune, for studies, though the term is still vague, and signs up for both the Oxford and the Cambridge Entrance exams, receiving syllabuses and sample papers. Tess continues to wear uniform, having nothing else and no time to use clothes-coupons, and goes every day to the British Museum Library. The uniform ensures a ticket although Tess isn't even a student yet. The big Reading Room under the dome, with black leather seats and desktops in star-formation, is still in disuse, and readers have to walk through to the North Library, a long rectangular room with parallel tables and lamplights. This becomes Tess's office, and will remain so until Tess leaves London twenty-two years later, long after the North Library is once again a room for rare books and the big round room under the dome reopened, the star-shaped rows much more cheerful in blue vinyl and readers increased a hundredfold. Tess reads all day, unknown bliss, haphazardly but hard.

At the centre table Tess chooses, sometimes opposite, sometimes next, sits the most beautiful young man Tess has ever seen, with a halo of curly black hair above staring blue eyes and a delicately curved up nose. A young Beethoven. Also using the Library as an office, there punctually at nine. Reading books in German and English and some other language. And Oscar Wilde in Spanish.

Tess has grown bolder in a few months and soon makes the advance, asking the young Beethoven about a German noun, with a capital like all German nouns, even with an article attached. Tess can't find that noun in any dictionary. Like Klappenschrank. The young man smiles and looks. Of course. Klopstock. A German poet. Tess feels an idiot.

But the young Beethoven is delighted. Men are always delighted when a girl can be taught, Tess has learnt that early. Coffee follows. Why Wilde in Spanish? In dialogue, easier to learn the language well. The young Beethoven is a Polish poet. A peasant poet, left the village early and became famous in Warsaw at eighteen, a sort of Polish Rimbaud. The only good Polish poet. The only good poet in fact, except perhaps Shakespeare, this said with laughter. Working on a PhD, whatever that is. The young Beethoven explains, and Tess at once decides to do one too later. Meetings become regular. The young Beethoven studied at St Andrew's, Scotland, during the war, having fallen seriously ill in Rumania while escaping from Poland and unfit for soldiering. The Polish Government in exile paid for St Andrew's. The Poles in exile, except for a few literary enemies, are proud of the young poet. Tess is proud of the young poet. The young poet is the most wonderful happening ever, talking about poetry all the time, about Polish, German, Spanish, English poetry, unlocking all that suppressed scribbling. Tess is still steeped in a mishmash of Whitman, Hopkins and T.S. Eliot. The young Beethoven gently introduces Tess to Donne, to Dylan Thomas, to David Gascoyne, and translates poems for Tess, full of angels and lakes and Polish lore and solemn prayers and satanic dream books. Soon Tess and the young Beethoven are lovers. The young Beethoven is twenty-nine. Called Janek.

Sean is dropped. Tess is turned out of the digs at Cromwell

138

Road for bringing men in, and moves to Kensington Gate, nearer to Janek's coffin of a room. Janek and Tess meet daily. Janek walks towards Tess along Queensgate and stops, with open arms. Tess is to come towards Janek, not Janek towards Tess. That's the way Janek is.

London is transformed. The red underground becomes blood thundering under London's skin. The precocious pale street lighting smiles up at a hundred maple leaves hanging like hands a hundred times along a hypnotism of masked porticoes. A street lamp is a gem on a quarter-cross or a guardian angel handlessly blessing the lovers' white flame's shout. The stuttering sky full of birds plucks the eyes like parchment. A sigh sprinkles the night and whispering shapes embrace and apprehend lisping syllables. Rain on pavements turns to crackling fires, heels in the silent street scatter images and Tess is filled with a fear of the love of conflict.

Tess is not ready for this. Tess must not once again be swallowed whole, must not again postpone studies. This is quite different from the awkward duty with Ian, the experimental curiosity with Jon J., the careless physical with Sean. But these have produced a crack, a dissociation of mental and physical, a clinical detachment haunting Tess throughout life until old age, when at last the old lady can face the detailed history of body and mind together, too late. Janek is a skilled lover but Tess, mystified, astonished, does not spontaneously desire, is slow to rousing. Perhaps Ian ruined Tess for ever. A sensual, intellectual, aesthetic love, deep and real and lasting, isn't that just as strong, since Eros dies anyway? Aesthetic love is a symptom of frigidity, sang Froid to H.D., especially with aesthetic peers, but then, Froid sang much cold-blooded garbage on women, and Tess has not been frigid with others, nor is there or will be any aesthetic rivalry, nor male putdown, only mutual wonder, so rare, nor does Tess need to assume the personae of goddesses, whores and frolics, nor does this aesthetic love cause suffering, at least for Tess. Still, the split has occurred, there is no dark Laurentian passion for Tess, sex not even in the head but nowhere much, how can that be? Perhaps Tess has placed Janek, or maybe Janek has, on a divine pedestal.

139

The Iron Curtain, so named by Churchill, descends over Eastern Europe after the Potsdam summit. Tess imagines millions of shop-blinds slamming down along the immense new frontier.

Suddenly Jim Hardy contacts Tess again and offers a job in the British zone of Vienna, on an allied paper. Vienna! Journalism! Tess is suddenly prepared once again to give up the studies. But Janek remonstrates. What about love? Just like Ian. Makes Tess feel guilty. Janek will always be very good at that. And what about those studies? In that order.

That's the way Janek is. Tess gives in, and will always give in on most things. Janek is right of course. Unlike the others. The others prevented the studies, Janek prevents the abandonment of studies.

Janek is introduced to mummy in Kensington Gate. Mummy is shy as usual and seems elsewhere, asks Tess to go to the depot in South London where the Holbein House stuff is stored, to take any books wanted but put the rest up for auction and share the money with Joanne, except for whatever the piano fetches, that is wholly Joanne's. Joanne, having spent the end of the war in Naples and learnt Italian, then in Colombo, is now demobbed and in Addis Ababa, on some grand job. Tess goes to the depot in the Old Kent Road, but saves only Pooh Bear and two narrow bookcases. Mummy is quite annoyed. The Lang Fairy Books, mummy says, those were very valuable.

But mummy, there's no room here.

Mummy asks if Tess intends to marry Janek. Tess doesn't know, Janek hasn't asked.

Janek is a Catholic, presumably?

Yes.

Does Tess know the Church's attitude to divorce?

Tess doesn't. Is shocked. Is shocked again by the Church's attitude to contraception. Curious being now shocked by conservative attitudes to things once shocking Tess. Curious how mummy now talks of things unmentionable before. Because Tess is a married woman. But Tess used contraceptives with Ian.

That's different. There was a war on.

Why different? Anyway Janek was married before, too.

Oh?

140

Yes, to a beautiful Armenian, in an Orthodox Church, just turn round three times and the marriage is over.

Don't be silly darling. That's the Mohammedans.

Anyway, the marriage to Ian was in an Anglican Church. If the Orthodox marriage doesn't count the Anglican shouldn't either.

Mais si, justement. The Catholic Church is in communion with the Church of England. Otherwise there wouldn't have been any SSC.

Tess can't follow these canonical subtleties, nor cares. Tess has no intention of becoming a Catholic.

Anyway Janek hasn't asked. Janek's quite happy as things are. Mummy sighs.

But Janek as a Catholic mustn't be led away from the fold.

The fold. Tess squirms at this rhetoric now.

And in fact Tess and Janek decide to live together, finding a cheap room at 9 Oakley Street, round the corner from Cheyne Walk where mummy now lives in that lay community. Back to SW3, but the pleasanter end, even if only in lodgings.

Janek not only does not hinder Tess but actively helps with all the preparation. Tess also counter-helps Janek on the thesis, a comparative study of English and Polish poetry from mediaeval to modern, and learns a lot. For Tess, though still ignorant, has acquired in BP a good editorial and analytic mind almost irrespective of subject-matter, whereas Janek, apart from writing in another tongue, is a poet, and tends to juxtapose beautiful but unlinked paragraphs. The argument isn't always clear. Is this a however-para or a moreover-para? This friendly collaboration will continue for years, long after both have written many books, and to the end Janek will show Tess every little thankyou note, though in perfect English.

Tess sits for the Oxford exam in April, in the Senate House Library under arranged supervision. There Tess bumps into Jane Shields again, briefly, now doing research, and is wished good luck. The Cambridge exam is in June, but Tess gets an interview at Somerville College in May, first with the English tutor, then with the principal Dr Janet Vaughan, a remarkable lady. Contrary to Tess's fears at having to explain the change of married name back to maiden, Dr Janet Vaughan is enchanted: a student already divorcing at twenty-three! This exam was specially devised for ex-service women, Dr Vaughan says, and ex-service women are not expected to be inexperienced schoolgirls.

Tess receives the telegram a week before the Cambridge exam and cancels. Why sit again when already offered a place? Thus are important choices made, out of laziness. The Labour Government is dishing out generous grants to ex-service people provided a place is obtained. The grant will pay all the fees and a bit more for vacation expenses, over three years, and the savings will look after clothes and books. Tess is all set. Tess has won. University wasn't even imaginable in 1939. Tess seems to have done well out of the war, had a good war in fact, smugly and with a pinch of shame, remembering tales of women's guiltily triumphant work and freedom, so threatening to the spurious heroism of men fast turned to mud, entrenched helplessness and shell shock, and at the cost, in the end, of over eight million dead European men and over thirty-seven million casualties in the First War.

Mummy is also all set, suddenly, announcing: this lay community is not enough.

Not enough? For what?

Well darling, just enough to learn to want the whole thing.

The whole – ?

To become a Benedictine.

A what?

Remember Tyburn Convent?

No.

Mother St Paul, sent that box of clothes.

Oh. Yes.

Well, Mother St Paul is dead now, but Tyburn kept in touch, and, well... Mummy is shy. Mummy has been accepted as a postulant.

A what?

A postulant. That's the name for the first year. After that the postulant becomes a novice, for three years.

But mummy, at fifty-two!

Yes, mummy says quietly. Called a late vocation.

But the hardship, the lack of freedom, the –

But mummy has been thinking about that for a long time.

142

Grandad left some money to all six children, and mummy's share will be handed over as dowry.

As dowry!

Stop repeating everything. But mummy speaks gently. The convent can't be expected to support a nun for life, there'd be far too many false vocations. Especially at fifty, perhaps less able to do tough work than the younger nuns.

Work!

Well of course. All the domestic tasks are shared out, in turn. Some Orders have much harder tasks. Religious Orders represent aspects of Christ's life, some teach, some heal and so on.

And what is this Order's task?

To pray.

Oh, Christ!

Don't swear, darling. Tyburn is an Enclosed Order. Perpetual Adoration, the Sacrament is permanently exposed, to two nuns perpetually praying for two hours at a time.

Tess is dismayed, stops arguing, can't see mummy kneeling for two hours, Tess's knees ache at the thought.

An Enclosed Order. What about visits?

Of course darling, often. In the parlour. Not behind a grid like the Carmelites.

Tess is silent. This is like death without the paraphernalia of death. But with the dowry of paraphernalia.

In August, Tess joins mummy in Luxemburg for a month, a last holiday together, arranged by the Voyages Blair and paid out of the future dowry. Janek is none too pleased, but the circumstances being exceptional, quenches the possessiveness,

Tess stops over in Brussels and gets all Tante Mathilde's anger about the dowry. The Catholic Church has always been rapacious and so on. Tess at once switches sides. And to change the subject produces a photograph of Janek taken on Hampstead Heath. In black and white.

Mais . . . Janek est un juif!

Tess is stunned by the tone, can hardly speak.

Of course not, Janek is of Lithuanian descent, from the North West of Poland.

Well, that wouldn't –

143

And if Janek were a Jew?

At once Tante Mathilde is on the defensive, didn't mean, of course, never, the Red Cross saved Jews and so on.

Why is Tess only now learning to rebel against the family? Joanne did so years ago, if aggressively and not over the same things. Tess does another side-switch, pro-Joanne.

In Luxemburg the remnants of the Siegfried Line can be seen across the Moselle during walks on wooded hills, and Tess tries again. Isn't mummy partly, deep down, doing this to be off Tess's and Joanne's hands?

Mummy denies this of course, Tess is independent now and Joanne is doing very well, on a top job in Abyssinia.

Not as independent as all that, only on a grant. Just suppose for a moment Tess had plenty of money, for say, a cottage and support, and mummy could have woody walks and go to Mass every day. Would mummy still go in?

Well...No...Yes...No...Yes, of course.

Tess is deeply disturbed by this answer. Mummy'll never stick the life.

But mummy retaliates uncertainties. Oxford, is Tess sure? Won't Tess feel outclassed? And Janek, so clever, etc.

Mummy goes in. Tess visits in Royston, a subsidiary house. The middle-aged postulant is wearing a shin-length black dress and a wide white veil, the grey hair still visible and as yet uncut. Keep getting the veil caught on rose-bushes in the garden, mummy says. The nuns are not allowed mirrors, and mummy borrows Tess's to have a looksee. Mummy misses cigarettes. Hasn't even been allowed to keep a silver thimble, given to Tess.

In September Churchill issues a call for a United States of Europe, to ensure peace. And, now the war is won, Tess supposes all nationalisms are over at last.

In October Tess starts a new life, in a modern semblance of a cloister, Somerville College, Oxford, where, in one of the small front-quad rooms allotted to the first year students, Tess tears up the studied studio photograph of the Army Captain and the Waaf Flight Officer, much to the lady-scout's wailed sorrow, a shame, ever so nice that, and settles to new friends and new horizons.

11. FILE: JANEK

Tess's split and scattered youth has so far been a peculiarly inadequate initiation to life. And the late-reached alma mater, like the mater, teaches little and Tess is obliged to learn alone. In a sense that's the idea: throw the students to the wolves. Or, for the mater: life (God, school, the firm, the government) will provide. The dreaming spires, though in a busy city, are still dreaming.

But the famed tutorial system, originally devised for an élite of young men to walk along the Isis with a tutor discussing Plato, is wholly unsuited to an ignorant girl straight from the Services. The tutor recommends certain lectures, but these are not compulsory, nor immediately relevant, nor part of an evaluation, and repeated year by year instead of being published, even, according to returning Service students, with the same jokes in the same places. The real teaching supposedly goes on in the tutorial, where the tutor merely sets an essay-subject, spends the next week's tutorial listening, says Very Interesting then demolishes the essay in a few well-chosen words.

This certainly trains students in small researches and perpetual writing. After three years of weekly essay-crises a girl is written out of gormless gushings and swiping generalizations, and suffers no block facing real research. And when the middle-aged professor in Paris tells complaining students – complaining about one essay and one exposé a term for the credit – how students then had to attend lectures and write an essay per week per tutor, and how that didn't even count, only the final exams counted, over ten days on the work of three years, there is mere disbelief, just a professor old-daysing away.

But the old days are not at all, for Tess, like the Oxford of

Hardy, even less like the Oxford of Beerbohm's *Zuleika Dobson* or Waugh's recently published *Brideshead Revisited*, the champagne dinners and the drunken orgies. Tess does try some of the many extracurricular activites, morning coffee at the Playhouse, where the current student idol, Pierce Wyngate in a purple suit, reigns like a cadaverous version of the young Sebastian Flyte; or the Union debates, one on the death of the novel, where the same Pierce Wyngate in a speech against the motion asks the entire assembly whether anyone has read Kafka, to be greeted with total silence then laughter as the point is made, while Tess, up in the women's gallery, hasn't the courage to say yes; or the innumerable clubs and societies representing every nuance of thought political, religious, historical, literary; or the teas and sherries in students' rooms at Balliol, Christchurch, Hertford et al. A student could be perpetually busy in Oxford yet not do a stroke of work.

And Tess works hard. But soon becomes rather like mummy in being somehow always elsewhere.

The first elsewhere is in time. After a term of disappointing tutorials, Tess insists on doing the mediaeval, philological course. The half-forgotten model Jonathan suddenly surges as modal for a noodle, most mentowers leaving muddled traces. A passion for language misleads Tess into interpreting the word Philology as the science of language, now called, unknown to Tess, Linguistics. Tess also feels, in this muddled modal, how anything from Shakespeare on can be read alone, especially under Janek's illuminating guidance. This unexpected chance of at last and after all attending a university must be used to read literature needing to be taught.

The English tutor demurs. Tess has a good critical mind, Tess will suffer.

Tess suffers. For the philology tutors are worse than the literary. The Anglo-Saxon Philology tutor talks way above Tess's head for the hour, about seventh-century palatalization, then tells Tess to read the chapter on palatalization in Luick's *Historische Grammatik der englischen Sprache*, a heavy tome all about vowels. And Tess daring to ask a question the next time is made to sink through the floor. Then the tutor talks for an hour about Anglian Smoothing, same scenario. Clearly undergraduates are the scum of the earth to this man, only interested in ninth-century Kentish glosses.

For of course, as Tess soon discovers, Philology is not the Science of Language but historical phonology, Verner's Law, Grimm's Law, not laws at all but one-time consonant-shifts from say *p* to *f* and *t* to *th* as in pater, or how palatal *a* was pronounced in eighth-century Mercian, and other such quagmires and quandaries for scholars to date and emend old texts. Perhaps the emenders on the Watch were philologists? Read Wright's Anglo-Saxon Grammar and start on *Beowulf* for next week. Probably, says Professor Wrenn lecturing on *Beowulf*, Grendel's mother had not read X's proposed emendation here. Read Sweet's Old Icelandic Grammar and start on the *Hrafnkelssaga* for next week. Tess can't read the grammar in a week so starts on the saga, and after looking up *ok* five times remembers *ok* as *and*. What would that form have been in Old Gothic, Miss Blair-Hayley? Or in Old Frisian? Tolkien in a seminar tells the story of a lady called Antrobus seeking a Greek etymology like *anthropos* for the name but given an Anglo-Saxon etymology instead, *anwintrigbur*, meaning one-year-old cow shed, then trying Tolkien's opposite number in Cambridge with the same result. Now work out the sound-changes involved. Miss Blair-Hayley? Read M.K. Pope's *From Latin to Modern French*. Tess wakes from dreams working out the detailed development through Gallo-Roman of Latin *manducare* to French *manger*. Luckily Old French is easier, and a delight.

Luckily also, the mediaeval literature tutor is a real teacher, young, enthusiastic, asking for essays beforehand and spending the hour in real discussion, essays on *Beowulf* (the hero leaping into the sea of the psyche to slay the minitaurus and disappearing), *Andreas* (much more exciting metaphors), *Sir Gawain* (ditto), or Langland where characters like Hunger and the Seven Deadly Sins are killed, the former by force-feeding, the latter by forced confession, the teacher never afraid to admit ignorance but jumping up to check. Good teachers, mind-openers instead of closers, are rare and fondly remembered. The old lady suddenly thinks of the history mistress in Brussels, with a lace handkerchief in one hand and spell-binding tales of ancient Greece in the other,

Tess always identifying with Athene. And the literature mistress teaching Verhaeren's *Le chaland* and *Le moulin*, now still recited in a trance.

But Tess does achieve, the hard way, that desire to know most European literature up to the fifteenth century fairly well, and does catch up with the rest, over many years, both alone and mentored by Janek. In fact at the moment Tess allows a vast gap between mediaeval and modern, plunged at one end in say *The Battle of Malden* and at the other, for leisure and pleasure, in Mallarmé and Eluard and Sartre and Greene and Waugh (astonished by the world of all those rich but silly people), though *Brideshead* does teach Tess more against the Catholic Church than all later instruction. And Janek reveals an unknown world of then unraved, offbeat works, Kafka, Hofmannsthal, Rilke, Stefan George, Sterne, Góngora and all Baroque, Perez de Ayala's *Tigre Juan*, printed in two columns, Ramón Gómez de la Serna's *Greguerías*, Gombrowicz's *Ferdydurke*, Choromaski's *Jealousy and Medicine*, the poetry of Cyprian Norwid and loopy tales by an Argentinian called Borges.

And there are unexpected compensations: Chaucer, found hard in the old correspondence course, is reached from behind, through eighth, ninth all the way to fourteenth-century English and French, and suddenly seems astonishingly modern.

Tess also acquires a deep sense of language. Philology is dry bones, but fillology slowly communicates magical seachanges, la mer la terre et l'air of a writer's material, the skeleton filling in with flesh and blood and sinews, molecules of desire, of creativity, vowels softening consonants, consonants breaking vowels, disappearing, changing places, becoming mute, still there as dried up foetuses in the spelling but unuttered, meanings accumulating, shifting into opposites, Frankish invading Gallo-Roman, Anglo-Saxon invading Celtic, Old Norse invading Anglo-Saxon, French invading English, Latin and Greek invading French and English, American invading French despite francophoney maniacs, the wheel coming full circle, enriching, cluttering, duplicating, complicating and simplifying the navigational skill of the language, language keeping the necessary, concealing the intake, throwing out the surplus back into the wine-dark sea, getting rid of the paraphernalia. Language is like Tess, absorbing alien elements and yet somehow always elsewhere.

The other elsewhere is in space. Tess rings Janek at ten every evening or vice versa as Tess waits in the college phone-box. Janek occasionally visits. Oxford is still very strict about men in rooms, students being in by ten, and other things. Tess once receives a note from the Bursar saying Tess was seen going into lectures wearing trousers under the gown, and red, at that! – in fact dark wine corduroy. But the terms last only eight weeks, and the vacations in the Oakley Street poor lodging are transforming, transliterating, transliberating. With each reunion Tess learns how absence must be abolished, lingering space lifted from a face, how lips can lepse and lapse in loops, how bones become ringing ivory telephones.

Janek and Tess are both unenglish, if in different ways, Janek impressing Tess with the prewar Central European popular songs of Zara Leander in German and *Gloomy Sunday* in Polish. But both share a foreignness and an orphan status, for Tess has no family in England other than an enclosed nun, and what's left of Janek's family is in Poland. No in-law problem.

Except Joanne. When Joanne returns from Abyssinia, jobless and broken by the end of a love affair, Tess is enthusiastic to help, suggests studying for a degree too, in French and Italian, gets the ministry man to agree about a late ex-service grant. But Joanne refuses, not clever like Tess, nobody needs a degree, nobody wants to live in a slum, like Tess. Tess sees the head of a fashion school, willing to take in Joanne though older. Same scorn. This is the last time Tess will ever interfere, though not the last time begged for help in trouble, with pages of accusations for interfering. Joanne does get jobs, always abroad, everything hunky-dory at first then everyone a sod and a bitch, followed by descents on London and demands.

But the least said about Joanne the better. Janek, though distantly polite, can't stand Joanne's insistent insensitivity, nor can any friends, even Joanne's friends. Exit Joanne, slamming doors to Tess's relief. Re-enter Joanne, re-exit ad infinitum.

The New Look splurges in, with long skirts, making hopeless demands on material, for clothes coupons and ration books continue, and Tess makes a new dress out of an old dressing-gown, ridiculous but creating a sensation in Oxford from mere novelty, and, at last, has made up the more elegant prewar red and gold brocade and blue taffeta from Ian's dead mother, for parties, no objection from Janek.

And slowly Tess counter-integrates Janek into English ways, including popular humour through the radio shows, Tommy Handley's ITMA, Ted Ray, Bernard Braden, Frankie Howerd. Both feel a shock when Tommy Handley dies suddenly and the next instalment of ITMA is nevertheless broadcast, a dead man's funny voice. Today the experience is routine, and visual. At that time, in Shaw's last years, Shaw plays can be seen everywhere in London, even *Back to Methusaleh* in three sessions at The Arts Theatre, two evenings and a matinée. Eventually too most of Shakespeare gets seen, and Ibsen, Strindberg, Sartre, Anouilh, later Beckett and Pinter and the new realistic drama of the fifties. The old Chelsea Classic Cinema is rediscovered with delight, all the famous French films not seen because of the war, and others. Living with Janek is an education. But Tess also begs to be taken, much later, to the Beatles at the Royal Command Performance.

There are, however, differences. Tess either gives in or keeps quiet. Janek doesn't like Janet and Jock, so Tess drops Janet and Jock. Janek isn't interested in music, so Tess cuts out music, despite the way Janek says every writer has either music or visual art as second love. But Tess is not a writer yet, though deep down unhappy then at the paradox of passionately writing bad poetry. There is so much else besides music: love, literature, exhibitions, the theatre, the cinema, dancing. Janek dances the samba like a Sambalese and takes Tess to nightclubs. Janek is always elegant, has only two suits but tailor-made, and full evening garb. Either Janek has mysterious sources of income as a graduate student on a Polish grant, writing for exile papers, or borrows from one to repay another, liking to appear lavish, with only unexpected meannesses.

The old lady's fingers are on the keyboard of memory. Suddenly, from the wedding and engagement ring on the left hand lurches a lost image. Walking on the Embankment one night, Janek asks Tess to stop wearing Ian's engagement and wedding

150

rings. Tess says these are a protection in Oxford, holding young men at a distance, for young men try to test Tess's fidelity, in vain. The current idol Pierce Wyngate once walks into Tess's room, saying Tess has been mentioned in *The Isis* as one of the three most beautiful women in Oxford, Wyngate has slept with the other two and wishes to complete. Tess doesn't read *The Isis* and shrugs Wyngate away with a laugh.

But Janek insists. So Tess throws the plain, single-diamond engagement ring into the glittering black Thames. That seems a good compromise, appeasing jealousy and superstition as well as satisfying usefulness. For when Tess and Janek marry in 1948 – no fuss, no presents, just two witnesses at the Registry Office – Janek can't afford a wedding-ring, so Tess keeps Ian's, but transfers the ring to the right hand, Polish custom. Janek seems content. That's the way Janek is.

And now, forty-five years later, the old lady remembers. The ring is still Ian's, transferred back to the left hand in Paris, Western custom, and later added to with a ring given by Vanna, an oval alexandrite surrounded by diamonds, to fake an original engagement ring. The alexandrite changes colour, blue-green in daylight, purple at dusk, dark pink amethyst in electric light.

The whole transaction now seems comically significant of something or other, Janek's firmly imposed but peculiar principles perhaps, or the astonishing peasant meanness surging up full force from under the noble generosity during the separation twenty years later, or the exemplary diplomacy Tess tried so hard to emulate, the other side of that being deviousness, or, why not, a secret wish of Janek's not to be truly married. Or maybe none of these things, just the original donor's magic ring, translocating Tess to the fortuitousness of an enchanting relationship.

However, the original donor has left not only the ring in inheritance, but also a fundamental atheism, added to the godless childhood, and a strong left-wing bias.

Janek is both deeply superstitious and religious. The superstitions seem harmless games, about zodiac signs, dates, and numbers, and an uncanny if sometime erroneous talent in thought-transference. Janek also loves to read hand-writings as a party-trick, not so much from graphology as from simply holding the letter, and achieves startling successes. Secretiveness too, and diplomatic evasiveness, seem part of the superstition. Never give anyone any information about anything, the information will be used or the thing won't come off. Never write an angry letter, the problem will go away. And indeed Tess does try, but mostly fails, to learn these lessons with Joanne. Never reveal failures or discouragements, people will believe those, rather than the successes, and of course Janek never does. Tess, when not simply silent and melding, has always been a blurter, like Joanne, and consulted people.

Janek seems suspicious of words, or perhaps just English words, rarely mentions love and makes love in silence, but writes a poem in Polish for Tess, called The Spelling of Love, long ecstatic variations on the letters L, O (O for Orion...) V, E. And suspicious of names: Janek never calls Tess Tess, or even Theresa like other friends, but Kotek, Polish for kitten. With friends, Janek often sits chin in hand, mumbling behind closed fist over the mouth, from shyness perhaps. Sometimes Tess feels haunted by some untold mystery of Janek's otherness. But that's the way Janek is.

This secretiveness is rather like mummy's, Tess feels, but shared, at least in appearance: an exclusion within a total mutual absorption, both temperamental recluses.

Religion is more serious. Janek is religious in an obscure poetic way, never mentioning God but introducing angels, saints and the Virgin Mary into some intangible but daily pantheon, like pagan idols. Neither Janek's nor mummy's pressure is ever insistent, but rather gently seductive with sweet certitudes, the greater the uncertainty the more infinite the infinity, the Greene Waugh fad full on, and Tess half becomes a half-willing Catholic, an aquaescence again, attending Mass every Sunday with Janek, balancing the halfness by making a poetic theme out of the conflict, pouring out dreadful poems about catechumens, guardian angels, satanic temptations and exorcisms. If Tess had nothing to say for Jock, Tess now has religion versus love to say, and pounces on that, but still has nothing to say.

For silent conflict there is. Tess's only way to face the flip-flop *fadeurs* of religious language is intellectual, and Tess plunges into

theology's quaint premiseless syllogisms for dogmas, say, of
bodies declared immaculate being ipso facto upwardly mobile,
and equally premiseless but more enticing heresies. Technically
Janek is living in sin with Tess. A beautiful, twenty-two year sin.
Tess even starts proceedings for an annulment in Rome, to free
Janek from Tess-imposed sin, through more flip-flop Farm Street
Jesuits and Vatican lawyers, proceedings based on half-lies by
everyone, even mummy, and continuing for years and years,
engulfing more and more of Tess's hard-won earnings. Ian at
first refuses to give evidence in a foreign court, evidence of
suicide threats, then finally turns friendly and complies. But
Janek seems to take all that in a metaphysical stride, watching
Tess's struggles with a mysterious detachment, as if Janek had
the key to paradise anyway, and couldn't be bothered with these
canonical subtleties. Janek's faith is primitive, deep and serene,
unobstacled by the deadening language of churchmen. That's the
way Janek is.

In any case Tess has always plunged, like a German Stuka. Into
the triangle of velocity, into the Wehrmacht and the Luftwaffe,
into mediaeval studies, into Polish, into Spanish, into classical
jazz, playing the records when Janek is out, into learning the
guitar for want of a piano, into pop song, into the poetry of Ezra
Pound, into Chinese ideograms to read Pound, into George
Eliot, George Gissing, into the books of Simone Weil – a model
of not belonging, a profound Christian convert but refusing
baptism to the end – into early linguistics, psychoanalysis, modern
French literature, philosophy, craning the skull almost off the
neck. The old lady's head is now a nuclear processing plant of lost
knowledges, acquired with immense efforts, sometimes leaking
or exploding and polluting, but now reduced to small clean
nuggets buried in deep salt caverns of the mind.

Marital breakfasts, unusually, are a dream-interpreting delight,
Janek preferring Jung, rich in self-evading poetic and religious
symbols, to Freud, and the Egyptian dream book to both, where
dreams are prophecies and confirmation of divine mystery. Tess,
though critical of all, is more down to earth. Yet blind neverthe-
less.

Janek is vain, and rightly so, needs six compliments a day but rarely pays any, and constant reassurance, especially after a party (was Janek all right?). Janek reproaches Tess for not being vain enough, not spending more time at the mirror, as other women do. Once, after tea in a smart Polish café, Janek scolds Tess for a shiny nose: ex-wife Danuta was there. Tess feels mortified. Why didn't Janek say? Janek did, kept repeating *czatka*. Tess has never heard this code-word before. That's the way Janek is.

The exile Poles are charming, but obsessed, naturally enough, with exile politics. When Janek starts publishing novels in English, the Poles say traitor. Slowly Tess weans Janek away. A mistake probably, but Janek is willingly weanable, changing from Polish to more universal topics. This is perhaps the only instance of Tess playing the Nanouk game, pulling Janek over rather than being nanouked over, as Tess usually was by Jean-Luc.

The old Professor of Polish at the Slavonic School of London University once invites Tess and Janek to an exile performance of Wyspiański's play *Wesele* in a big theatre. Tess has learnt enough Polish and knows the play fairly well, Janek having explained the play scene by scene. But the Professor insists on translating loudly for Tess, much to the annoyance of the Poles around, and Tess's silent fury. Even at the symbolic moment when the cock crows the Professor leans over and hugely whispers: THE COCK CROWS.

Some Poles clearly think Tess is not a good thing for Janek. But then, some English think Janek is not a good thing for Tess. Yet Janek and Tess impress as the perfect couple, exuding joy, this strange Pole, this enthusiastic girl.

Years later, when half-alienated in France, the old lady begins to understand the wrenches of Janek's inner transformations, from poetry to prose, like Tess but good poetry, from Polish to English, like Tess from earlier French but unwritten in, from eternal student to responsible professor, like Tess. And understands, too, Janek's weird suspicions of the English, so subtly arrogant and oneupmanshiply. The English friends Janek and Tess meet – poets, painters, professors, publishers and pundits, lawyers and lecturers, writers and psychoanalysts – always seem to have money as backing: when an Englishman is broke, says Janek, that means investments can't be got at or an overdraft

154

must be increased. The old lady has a flash of Janek endlessly and nervously counting and recounting small change. What? says Janek when a couple splits up, the wife keeps the house? Tess explains, the house could well belong to the wife anyway. How very English, Janek says, parents give houses as wedding-presents. When the husband of a friendly couple pays court to Tess Janek says how very English, instead of just human. Janek's integration is slow. The position of exile in an alien society, the old lady now reflects, is a bit like the position of women in a male society, except women are taught early to aquaesce.

The politics, from the start, are not those of Tess, but this never matters since Tess never talks politics. But Janek does teach Tess a great deal, long before the Goulag was known as such or even admitted by left-wing intellectuals, about Communism, political prisoners and Russian labour camps, where many Poles suffered for years, Tess reading several books by escaped Poles with horror. Paradoxically, considering how little the West did for Poland, even moving the guaranteed frontiers and occasioning mass deportations of peoples from East to West, Janek somehow expects the West to go to war at every Communist takeover, from the Czech putsch in 1948 to Hungary in 1956 and Prague in 1968, instead of turning blind eyes.

After the Oxford degree in 1949, Dr Janet Vaughan introduces Tess to a BBC head-hunter, to train as producer, but Tess goes doggedly on to a PhD in London. Janek is surprised, but loyally concurs. Janek, unusually for the time, fully accepts intellectual autonomy for Tess. The danger is of two autonomies perhaps. An inkling too dim to speak of is pushing Tess, the memory of mummy at forty-three without qualifications in the thirties slump.

But there are still inequalities, forgotten today, taken for granted then. The grant is extended but considerably reduced because Tess now has a husband, and a husband supports. Tess, self-supporting now for nearly ten years, finds this notion as quaint as the Unpaid Domestic for a diplomat's wife. Tess asks archly if a male student getting married also gets the grant reduced. In vain. Tess starts reviewing books, but earns very little, though receives unexpected sums, twice, from a lost godfather in Geneva, and another from selling those shares in the resuscitated Medical

Addressograph Company, so does manage to contribute here and there, not to mention endless pre-synthetics services as sock-darner and shirt-scrubber and ironer, and is self-supporting as to looks and books. Janek is now teaching at the Slavonic School of London University, but in a lowly capacity, giving intensive courses in Polish to officers, and correcting great wads of A-level Polish summer after summer to pay for holidays. Slimak's attitude to the squire was enormous, writes a candidate, and this phrase is delightedly adopted as rare expression of love. For years Janek will be excluded from academic teaching by nationality, even made to compete for a post with a research student directed by Janek as the only person qualified. Out of pride Janek refuses to apply, but Tess, indignant, pushes Janek and good sense finally prevails. Janek gets the post, and changes nationality afterwards. Today Polish names, descending from that exiled generation, appear in TV credits or as lawyers and journalists and doctors, and those methods are now only applied to qualified blacks and Indians and Pakistanis, unless needed for the National Health Service.

During the PhD, Tess's supervisor sends all the boy graduate students for interviews, but not Tess. Tess, indignant only on Janek's behalf, takes this as fact of life. And later, when really needing a job, Tess modestly applies for bottom-grade university posts, but is too qualified, with a PhD and a critical book, and when applying higher up has no teaching experience. Gone are the magic sesames of the war. So Tess drifts into literary journalism, soon graduating to the posh papers, and, at last, to novels.

For Janek and Tess are indeed very poor, living for fifteen years in a rent-controlled room and a half, with gas-ring on the floor until Tess buys a stove and puts in a sink, and a freezing bathroom on a stick-out back-landing shared with other lodgers. But intellectuals lived much more humbly in the fifties than later. Invitations could mean just wine. One memorable evening there was a game of poetic consequences, with each writing a couplet plus one line, folding over just before that line, and each then having to rhyme that line and add another. The results, especially with poets like Burns Singer and Sydney Graham there, were surrealistic. Burns Singer seems not to like Tess and when in cups deviously suggests Tess is bad for Janek, trying to be a rival, but this Tess does not believe. A few streets away the critic George Fraser holds poetry readings, each bringing a bottle, gentle George insisting in vino veritas: Tess's poetry is bad. The put-down comes from others, never from Janek. Tess knows or half-knows, but is learning to use words, and in a few years will fulfil that eighteen-year-old vow and produce a first novel, never writing another line of verse. There is advantage in belatedness. Because of a glamour photograph the novel is reviewed with Françoise Sagan under the rubric 'The teen-age tribe', though Tess is then thirty-four. And every Sunday Tess and Janek met the local literati at the Embankment pub. Publishers' parties were grander but writers were never made to feel poor, though a publisher later lunching Tess as author always provoked the silent question of why the money could not be simply handed over to pay for paper and pens and typewriter ribbon.

Summer travel is the top priority from the start, the first post-war adventure to Paris in '47, where Jean Marais is seen in a ludicrous translation of *Pygmalion*, no equivalent to Cockney being attempted, not even parigot, the lines 'The rain in Spain...' rendered literally, with 'Hampshire, Hertfordshire and Harwich' coming out with aspirated h's in Honfleur, Le Havre and Hyères. The next year to Geneva and the family chalet facing the Mont Blanc. But very soon to Spain, Janek's second foreign love, long before the touristic invasion. Janek still has a stateless passport, and Tess is quietly distressed to receive only a stateless sheet of paper. Tess has had a British passport since the age of thirteen, but is silent, puzzled by the distress, as with the pain at mummy's long expected death thirty-four years later. Tess has never belonged anywhere, yet feels this loss of official identity. The war, perhaps, made Tess half British. Or else the distress is due to the sexism, a word and concept then unknown, of the piece of paper.

And holidays soon become joint writing-expeditions, sitting at café-tables, still wrapped in two mutually respected concentrations at meals and not expecting witty entertainment, but reading chapters aloud in the evening for a first reaction. Further and further, more and more varied travel, by train or plane, later by car, all over Europe and more and more books. Thoth as alternative god, writing as ringwit, to outwit the inwit.

In the mid-fifties Janek has moved heaven and Communist burocracy to invite Jadwiga, a much older sister not seen since before the war, to Vienna. Jadwiga is about as old as the century, and should remember Poland in the interwar years. But is amazed: thinks all the cars must be official cars, and the gold and plush Café Mozart state-owned. Then, when lost in a poorer area the trio goes into a shabby little café, Jadwiga looks round and asks: so this must be state-owned? Just as, during the war, nobody could remember what a lot of butter looked like, humans infinitely adaptable and forgetful.

But Janek is possessive. Early in the research Tess is invited to Salzburg for a month's seminar. What, alone? Tess goes, perhaps the only instance of self-assertion. And when Tess returns and someone sends some photographs, Janek goes into a long meditation of erroneous thought-transference and accuses Tess of cheating, meaning infidelity. But there was no Flemish grammar-book on the seat.

Perhaps that is the moment when trust is first lost.

True, Tess later strains at the bit a bit, in this cloistered completeness, this leaning ivory tower, and needs other mentors, more rational if cruder, for another separate, disabsorbed, unstifled self, and after trust is lost anyway (perhaps the fifties were really the beginning of the end, unknown to Tess?), discovering with astonishment how men with nice but unintellectual wives also need mentors, or rather, intelligent women friends, rather than the physical outlets of the cliché: teas and lunches with British Museum readers and such. Tess is well aware of the sexual undercurrent in these intellectual binges, the undercurrent perhaps remaining under chiefly because these mentors, these diminished don Juans, are poor and married, and there's nowhere to go. One of these does become a long flirtation game, whereupon Janek vanishes into a full-blown affair. But the crisis passes. Tess is driven perhaps, by a hunger for rarely given compliments. Janek however insists on the marriage-relationship being very special. Together a tank, Janek says, rather oddly for a mystical person. And any other relationship, however innocent, is like a transfuge, subtly undermining that uniqueness. Tess had supposed a strong marriage could take such visitations in a healthy stride, especially with Janek's own outrageous flirtations at parties, ignored by Tess. Tess is not jealous or suspicious by nature. Perhaps that's the sufficiency Janek can't forgive. Tess gives in of course, after such an appeal. But will nevertheless pay for these intellectual infidelities one day, out of all proportion, at first only with the loss of trust. The day when Tess has removed the portraits of Janek's parents from the wall for framing in old gold as birthday present, Janek notices at once, accusing Tess as jealous iconoclast. And the old lady has never forgotten Janek's look of glaring suspicion when coming in one day to find Tess on the phone receiving the news of Burns Singer's death. Jimmy's dead, Tess says in answer to the glare and bursts into tears.

During these mild marital conflicts Tess suddenly remembers aunt Dorothy's letter, and plunges again, in the late fifties, from reference to reference, into daddy's life. Tess has now read enough Freud to understand the plunge, but plunges all the same. A huge father-file accumulates, and then a novel, borrowing Ian's personality to become a son discovering a father, affection-ately reconstructing Alfred Hayley, not a Jewish name after all, even less the Hayleys of Nairn, but a simple family of Anglican Warwickshire farmers.

In 1898, Alfred Hayley at twenty-two joins a small group of young men on the Isle of Dogs (*dogs?*), self-declared High Angli-can Benedictine monks, but steals a benevolent canon's books and a jewel from the cross. The case is reported briefly in *The Times*, hugely in the Church papers.

Tess is amazed. All those quaint clerical feuds, about the East-ward position, the Latin, the Gregorian chant, the nature of the Sacrament, the infallibility of the Pope and all the rest, only to be abolished sixty years later by Vatican II, at least for the unessentials, Masses now like Protestant services, with dreary hymns.

The lowish Church judge condemns Alfred to three years in Parkhurst. On coming out at the turn of the century, Alfred becomes a Catholic, goes to America, marries, and trades timber in Alabama. Tess contacts everyone just in time, the monks of Prinknash – for the original Order became very grand and too

Roman to remain in the Anglican Church – the mistress, the partners at the Addressograph Company, friends of the first wife in Mobile Alabama, an old carpenter in the Warwickshire village, even Aunt Dorothy, winsome and spiteful and still a sponger, and delightful old Florence Moss, up in the Potteries, Dorothy's governess in the nineties though only a year older, and learns how different old ages can be. Valéry or someone said any person is responsible for the face acquired by forty. But Tess knows already how and why any person is responsible for the kind of old age reached.

Tess is chiefly fascinated by two main features. First, daddy became a Roman Catholic, and divorced, furious with the Church for not recognizing the second marriage, yet influencing mummy towards the Church. Mummy confirms. Could daddy have insisted on Joanne and Tess being brought up as lapsed Catholics? Tess doesn't ask. Second, an astonishing pattern emerges: a Benedictine monk at one end, a Benedictine nun at the other, neither knowing those facts, and two children in between. No wonder Tess has strained. After the book, Tess no longer strains. God has become not only a manner of speaking but a self-righteous manner.

But illness pursues Tess, from the start, the same illness, always after intensive sex. Gradually Janek will also make the link, and gently leave Tess the initiative, a mistake, for Tess rarely takes the initiative, would prefer being ill if Janek did. Clearly also Janek needs more, and will find more, tells Tess shyly to read the Kama Sutra. Tess does, in the British Museum, and clucks at the clucking and the positions recommended. Tess is so in love, doesn't see the warning signs, assuming spirit will conquer all. And spirit does no such thing.

And when at last, in 1961, both having saved and saved, Janek and Tess acquire a flat in Hampstead, with a fridge! a bathroom! and a view over the whole of London, the roof-flat floating on trees, everything starts going wrong.

There's a New Year party at the Empsons, down the road. Towards midnight Tess goes up to Janek, feeling ill, and asks to be taken home to see the New Year in there. Janek is flirting. Tess leaves and trudges up the hill in the snow. Just before midnight

Janek arrives, panting. The next day Tess has a roaring temperature and is rushed to hospital. The sulphonomides of fifteen years ago have developed into innumerable antibiotics, but already create resistance. After six months in and out, Tess goes with Janek on holiday, to Vanna in Grasse, and there loses a kidney, is looked after by Vanna for six months, managing somehow to travel to Rome for a hilarious hearing before three priests in the Sacred Rota (ah si, conosco, says the chief priest, after asking for a description of a Dutch cap), is fetched by Janek at Christmas and goes back into a different hospital.

As Tess slowly recovers, Janek falls ill, has the gall-bladder needlessly removed but continues unable to digest anything, going to lectures with a zinging headache. Nothing organically wrong, that routine phrase, meaning nothing is visible on X-rays. At last the cause is found, an enzyme malfunction, rare but incurable. No diet advice is given, and several years of trial and error follow: Tess tries vegetarian only, white meat only, fish only, porridge only, but in fact, as Tess slowly comes to understand, nothing with fibres or grains will pass, nor of course fat, nor alcohol, nor red wine, and Janek is finally reduced to boiled potatoes, with champagne to enliven, and becomes the toast of London literary circles. Potatoes, the peasant, champagne, the sophisticated poet. The British Health Service, such a generous idea in 1945, put both Tess and Janek in a state unable to cope with a banal midlife crisis, and became the main reason why Tess did not return to England on retirement. And now the Health Service is in even deeper disarray.

The old lady reflects. Not the thrifty, threepenny thirties, not the fighting forties, not the fallow fifties, but the swinging sixties, this was the worst decade for Tess, and presumably for Janek. From the moment a real home and a Chair and literary success of a kind are achieved, everything crumbles. L'argent, l'amour, la forme, says a TV ad, Madame Soleil dira tout sur Minitel 3615 Soleil.

Apart from the new flat, the only two good points about the sixties are first, Tess's literary turning-point, after illness and meditation, in a more experimental, less popular direction, as if near-death had let the near-past die and strained backwards to early poetry and forwards towards renewal, inviting, inventing the future in a deep anxiety. Slowly Tess writes a completely different novel, and then two more, all three quite different from the swift first four and from each other, told over and over about barking up wrong trees, though the first two win prizes. But then the time is unpropitious, even to the great: when Tess had asked the then head of Faber and Faber, at a party in the late fifties, why the firm did not publish Beckett's novels as well as the successful plays the answer was: wouldn't touch those with a barge-pole. And second, buying an old car with a Travelling Prize, and both learning to drive, late in life. An inkling? The final escape four years later with a carful of books to Paris, not in a tank but in a second-hand Caravelle, bought with a publisher's advance for a book as yet to be written, is the first taste of sad yet elated independence.

For the tank blows up, as in old newsreels, together with the students in Paris and the Czechs in Prague, in great pain. Janek, caught in flagrant contradiction of a firmly imposed principle, yet fighting for manhood, reveals an unknown Slav cruelty, enforcing jealousy by unhealthily asking, after each weekend away, if Tess has suffered. Janek thought of Tess, says Janek. But embarks on a slow yet thorough demolition job, piece by piece, upon Tess's idea of Tess, no longer the helpmeet but the castratrix, dissimultaneously tried for reason by unreason, Janek also crashing from the pedestal thereby. A self Tess will have to reconstruct in Paris, piece by piece. But then, the old lady corrects, doesn't any attempt to tell such paraphernalia become a shuffled, redistributed pack of lies?

The annulment finally and uselessly arrives from Rome, saving Tess from another belonging. Tess has no objection to men's desires being cast everywhere and over aeons as God, only to what institutions have done to the idea of God. The beautiful twenty-two year sin comes to an end.

The only droll memories the old lady has are two. The first is of reviewing Simone de Beauvoir's *La femme rompue* for *The Times*, saying how women's magazinish, with tears nevertheless streaming down, and delivering the review by taxi for the deadline, in dark glasses to hide the swollen eyes.

The second is the sudden visit of Aunt Alice from Richmond VA, now on a widow's cruise to Europe with a friend, a vague Blair cousin called Katherine, also from Virginia. In mid-marriage crisis Tess has to drive these two to Sussex to see mummy. The vague cousin keeps making antediluvian remarks, about the Whites now having to pay for private schools. Why? Tess asks, knowing why. Well, to avoid the new mixed schools, Aunt Alice explains patiently. Aunt Alice never forgave the Blairs of Maryland for being on the Northern side. Katherine is descended from Princess Pokahontas, Aunt Alice says by way of atonement. Oh, says Tess, so Indian blood is okay? Well, yes. Why? Well, the Indians were very noble. So were the Blacks before being enslaved. Of course, Alice pursues, not hearing in the engine-noise, that was before the Indians started mixing with the niggers, and spoilt. The niggers are stoopid and lazy. Gee, says the vague cousin later, on films, how kinduv nice to see Anglo-Saxon names on the credits again. Oh, says Tess wickedly, names like Beowulf, Hrothgar, Wiglaf? The vague cousin is silent. The vague cousin clearly thinks Tess ill brought-up. Aunt Alice wants to visit Knole. Someone has said Knole is a must. In the portrait gallery the guide says That's Queen Elizabeth. That's Sir Philip Sidney. That's Archbishop Cranmer. Oh yea, says Aunt Alice, Cranmer died.

Aunt Alice also dies a few years later.

The Paris job falls upon Tess like manna in mid-wilderness. The student revolts of '68 have produced a new university in Paris, and Tess is invited by Janine, a French fan, deep Derridean and luring Lacanian, to teach there. The inkling, so dim thirty years earlier, has hey presto turned up trumps, not for those eight years of mediaeval studies, never used and now forgotten, but thanks to the PhD and publications. Dim inklings have some use for Tess goes straight to the top, despite all those job refusals in England's fifties for lack of experience, and leaves in a second-hand car bought with a publisher's advance, after a last weird fuss of Janek's about Tess taking minimum books to teach with, though the books belong to Tess, thankful there are no children to quarrel over. Perhaps books represent what had been shared, as children do. Tess leaves, ostensibly for a year's separation, the year lurching into seven, full of meetings and ditherings to a divorce, but ultimately ending after twenty-five years in a fragile rediscovery of a forty-five year friendship. The tip of Dubcek's shoe re-expanded.

Tess joins the '68 generation, the teachers all twenty or thirty, the students all ages but mostly very young, Tess now forty-five, slimmed by illness and crisis, rejuvenated by freedom, excitement, hormones after a hysterectomy (oof!) and permanent contact with the young. A second career, a second life.

12. FILE: OMEGA

Hello, Tess.

Hi, ole lady. Writing nicely?

Nicely, how tell? But writing. Is the portrayal a betrayal?

Always is. For others especially, somewhat summary.

Bifografy's like that. Can't invent, can't be free to go inside. All the main characters male or female, the mentors, are called John, for that reason.

And John began as a Chomsky rule about reflexivization. Is that why there are no pronouns?

Well, no personal pronouns, or possessives. Except of course in the diary, for contrast. Hard to do. For distance. A repossession after dispossession.

But there are ellipses, old lady.

Millions. The ellipses alone could make another story, an alternative history.

But why?

Memory's such a variable geometry. Just think, Tess, the first twenty-three years so starkly crammed and anecdotal, the second twenty-two years, one chapter.

That's the rhythm of life, old Houyhnhnm, slow, then faster and faster.

An unhelpful clayshit. All that shared happiness and productivity, so real, yet a non-narrative.

Perhaps because already narrativized, however indirectly. Anyway the labyrinth of married love isn't a plot, old thing. Someone said reality consists of non-events, history is about what goes wrong.

Oh, history. A sorry series of sad remakes.

But there were personal events, old lady, new friends, interesting encounters, publications, promotions.

That's the point in literary autobio when the author starts mentioning each book, what about, how written, how received, quibbling still with reviewers,and dropping names of all the known and lesser known come across. Is Tess angry?

No-o.

If an author survives at all, that sort of thing gets known anyway, others provide, producing something quite other. And if not, why bother?

Whereas nobody else can provide an unknown childhood and youth?

Look at the morning winter sun bronzing the cutback vines and silvering the cherrytree branches... Strange how nebulous and unnarrative publication and success and failure seem, from this end, so important at the time. Personal relationships, like politics, consist of constantly orbiting blind spots.

And then? As John the young script-writer would say. The next twenty years. The second life. Fled by like a TGV?

With many new friends, yet few memories, as age advances. The bewilderment at first, the endless meetings, the astonishing rudeness and chaos among colleagues, followed by friendly lunches, la bouffe rated higher than ideology. Every pedagogic problem politicized in a blind fanaticism of Gauchistes and Communists, everyone having to speak, in several points premièrement deuxièmement troisièmement and subpoints a,b,c,d and long subordinate clauses and sudden *d'autre part* and *par ailleurs* whenever the end seems in sight, so nothing is ever concluded.

Tout marche très bien en Chine, says Janine the deep Derridean in those early days, remember? Looking like Queen Nefertiti, in Cardin clothes and a luxury flat, unimaginable as intellectual sent to pick rice in mid Cultural Revolution.

Don't be mean, Tess. All the French intellectuals were confused.

Yet arch-convinced.

And by the eighties even the starry-eyed young teachers at last recover from réunionite to get on with the neglected Thèse d'Etat, and the Communists win, there is a Communist president of the University, teachers are obedient apparatchiks. Presumably that's how people drift into dictatorship, from sheer weariness at inefficient democracy. But many shifting discourses towards the

166

end – at least, the old lady left before the Wall fall and final system-collapse.

Nothing else?

The joys and difficulties of independence. All decisions to be taken alone and no sharing of delights. A few light love affairs at first, for self-convince and pleasure found again, never with colleagues and chiefly on holiday abroad, soon abandoned. Premen tension, postmen fatigue, nomen relief. Nay nor women neither, no rebound tendencies that way, except as friends. Men are afraid of strength, and Tess by force of circumstances becomes strong, accepting the reproach this brings. John returning silently to give Tess a tessness, a texture. And Tess enjoys teaching, a wholly new experience, if unsettling at first, with strikes and demos and invasions of classes. Dégueulasse, says an early student that first term, at something Tess has said. Say that in English, Tess replies with cool sangfroid, remember?

And then writes SHIT on the board, and the other students laugh. A dirty trick but silencing.

The hilobrow split unsplit, the canon crushed. Yes, Tess has to learn, learning also from students. But these eventually settle down, changing in one decade to much duller diploma-bent goody-goodies saying oui madame. The best classes are nevertheless the graduate seminars in literary theory. For Tess plunges as usual. Into Structuralism and Poststructuralism at the same time, teaching the first to the young, the second to the older. And into modern linguistics, –

At last! says Tess.

– philosophy, feminism, science fiction, the fantastic, everything, French popsong, tennis tournaments on TV, politics... Just when Tess has lost the right to vote anywhere, though paying taxes in France, the Boston Teaparty long forgotten. The second life is a vicarious public life, an opening out. Mental horizons are stretched like elastic, painfully, pleasurably, despite deep distrust of the French mania for systems, ephemeral but exciting. The lost wonder returns. But to Tess alone now. The mentors are all safely in print, Derrida, Barthes, Kristeva, Cixous, Irigaray, Foucault, Lacan, Bakhtin, Deleuze , Baudrillard and all the other maîtres-à-penser. Such an odd phrase.

167

Yes, very followistic, like the prêt-à-penser demanded by the students. Difficult, what with the war on the bien-pensants and constant deconstruction and chaos theory.

And in fact Tess works hard as usual, even on vacation, producing articles and critical books, making a new academic reputation and being invited to conferences or as guest-professor or on lecture-trips all over the States.

But also, Tess breaks in a bit indignantly, stranger and stranger novels, merry word-games, going regularly to the Pound castle to write.

Further up the Adige valley there is a little chapel called St Proculus, with ninth-century frescoes painted by Irish monks, and one of these shows God sending a shower of arrows down, remember? And the Virgin Mary protects St Proculus under a large blue cloak, the cloak sending all the arrows back to God.

Like early starwars. Thousands of such experiences, why not write all that up?

Oh, biofatigue. Much would be mere travelogue and international social comment, superficial at best. In a film there's nine days of shooting for nine minutes of screening, and many times more for a few minutes of special effects, in other words lovely lies. Besides, old people are of no interest, have only walk-on parts in most stories. And new acquisitions of knowledge after the Bildung part are a non-starter in narrative. What is knowledge anyway? Pleasure of the moment, then all for the worms.

Well in that light so is everything, and in five million years the sun will have swallowed the Milky Way or whatever. Come on old lady, no terminal blues just yet. What about –

So astonishing, how elements of pure chance, rather than, or maybe as well as merit, can govern a life. Being born in a non-calamitous zone, class and race, receiving three languages on a plate (well, one on a saucer) and three more through circumstances, though not kept up. Never facing the dole queues so dreaded by mummy, thanks to a murderous yet instructive war. Surviving. Meeting a wondrous partner in a library. Getting a government-paid education long before grants were cut or turned into loans. Citizen of an age when feminine autonomy was not only possible but becoming almost normal, at least for

168

those evading the boastmod bully backlash. Never tempted by drugs, alcohol, yachts, mink coats, jewellery and other paradis artificiels. Having all sexual experience between VD and AIDS. Never being a battered woman or a single parent. Able to keep that rabbit-hole vow, and even if people stop reading altogether, preferring knowledge and pleasure from a screen, those books were a joy to write, like tending vines and cherry-trees. Landing a top-job late in life when universities were expanding, able to prepare a sunny solitudinous old age. Ending up as a harmonious Houyhnhnm, invisible as old, as woman, as English to the French and vice versa, as offbeat novelist barking up the wrong tree, become the tree of life, and unlike most feminists enjoying that invisibility as a kind of enclosed order, preparing for the final invisibility. All this hypes humility.

Not mummy's daughter for nothing.

Not quite. Much more important are the many new friends. And the refriending with Janek, many years later, with visits and frequent phone-calls.

But with little in common now.

Janek, looking like a slim (on that diet) grey-haired prophet rather than a young Beethoven, seems repeat seems to have changed little, whereas Tess has become quite other, Apolline to Janek's Dionysus, secularized and disenfranchised. During the tankburst of mutual accusations, two softer things were said. The first, Janek wants to be adored. Adoration is for the gods, Tess replies, love for men.

Though Tess's own seeking of compliments elsewhere is an inferior version of the same human longing.

Second, what Janek most loved about Tess was forming Tess.

But Tess had loved the man not the pygmalion, all that sharing of knowledge was just an extra bonus, besides, Tess also formed and gave, of English ways and manners and syntax. Somewhere along the line Tess escaped that demand for adoration and that old formation impulse, becoming Tess.

The problem was oddly Jamesian – or Whartonian or later Catherian. Why did so many turn-of-the-century writers represent strength and creativity as an incubus, inevitably weakening the other, as if consisting only of a limited quantity weighted on scales going down or up on one side only? Wasn't equality in two internourishing autonomies within partnership also conceivable, as Tess thought had been achieved with Janek? Perhaps mentors are also guardian angels, even when destructive.

Yet all that still goes on, old lady, human, not temporal.

Tess and Janek do have one new feature deeply in common though: both are now living out old age, alone and separately, with many but mostly different friends, in unnative lands, writing in unnative languages, unbelonging to the last.

So the old Houyhnhnm wouldn't like to be young today?

No and no. Even diplomas lead to unemployment now. On a radio-discussion the other day about technology and unemployment someone used the cruel phrase le banquet des survivants. Untaken up. Clearly the century, if perhaps not yet the world, is ending on a whimper after all, rather than the long expected bang. Perhaps even the whimper is simulated. Symbols have replaced reality. Lenin statues pulled down, African soldiers in Western uniforms doing the goose-step – the goose-step! – imitating the Russians imitating the Prussians. A Nigerian in full-bottomed wig taking the oath to the next dictator. Judges walking in full regalia upholding the torn miscarried honour of British or other justice. Parades and pageants.

But things were always like that, merely more obvious to all now, isn't that an improvement?

After the psychedelic seventies, the yuppy yeighties, now the non-plussed nineties, though no doubt Big Joy will be organized for the Millennium, to celebrate the world's reentry into the Middle Ages, so ardently and blindly studied for eight years years ago as beauty rather than barbarism.

Unless humanity creates, as humanity often does, an unforeseen wonder.

Always the optimist, Tess, thank you, how right. This from the harmonious Houyhnhnm. But the remake is finished, even if more could always be added.

The old lady meditates.

Memory is not after all a computer, nor, a fortiori, a diskette or even a card-index, cards crushed between coloured tabs in long boxes and manually filled in, manually consulted, crushed again, out of sight. Like index-cards but swifter, the computer has memories but no sense of time, only data-banks, retrieved only if fed in at this or that moment. The computer can restitute three-dimensional images of lost architectural wonders or constitute future marvels, but these are hard-worked simulations, virtual reality. The computer does not see or smell or hear or touch or taste the world, the computer uses the present, each memory effaced by a second's hiccup of electricity or by the next operation unless stored, called up, the reference printed from the buffer memory. But the human buffer? Is memory present to memory?

Nor is memory like a book, for although old books have the smell and the feel of paper and print and leather, the smells and feels and tastes and sounds named by the words can never, as an image can to the inner eye, be brought to life in nostrils, fingers, tongue and ear, and Proust's little madlanes of memory can only name, however convolutedly, the reader maybe recalling something quite else.

Memory is not like a film either. Films are concocted with all those assistant-cutters, make-up designers, lighting engineers and focus-pullers, where every angle is pre-fixed, with flashbacks to precolour periods done in black and white or sepia. Most films today seem to be shot in black and infra-red anyway. Seeing an old film means seeing shots forgotten but the same shots, sealed in celluloid for ever. But an image in memory may be different each time and suddenly aggregate others. Nor is memory a telefilm, a newsreel or telenews, all prearranged as in fiction. All that guff at the beginning of the plunge into memory was a framed resistance to the plunge.

Chance, evaded by the human sciences imposing pseudo-systems, is at the heart of biology, of life. Memory is unique, random and fragile, like life, and like life dies for ever.

The old lady has been rereading that pink-saliented review of literary theory, an article about Point of View in film, the quick pick-up by early mass audiences of cuts from gaze-shot to object-shot explained by the child following the mother's gaze to what the mother is seeing, in primitive tribes, the Pokkot tribe for example. The old lady does not belong to the Pokkot tribe, and the theory does not seem to apply to babies strapped all day to the mother's back. Tess, though not strapped, did not follow the mother's gaze, the mother's gaze followed Tess from a photograph on the wall while the real mother gazed inwardly or at nothing. Hence Tess's early inability to be as clever as mass audiences

Memory is necessarily self-centred. For other people are fogs, alter ego et galore. Memory does not reconstruct points of view, only personal reactions, and all portrayal is betrayal. Only art reconstructs points of view, artificially, the novel, the film, the play, the staged confrontational interview. In memory all the parts are played by actors called John, in self-confrontation. And memory can invent memories.

Memory can quantum along from notion to notion. The meeting of particles are events and vice versa. The void before the Big Bang is a nil mass not a nothingness, the void has a structure, and gets transformed. But memory is not an accelerator of particles either.

Nor is memory a digging, a fishing, a lucky dip or a pinball machine, or a sundial showing only the light hours.

Memory is more like intercepting and decrypting, thousands of messages missed, or captured but not decrypted, and even the captured and decrypted now burnt or not released. Memory intercepts the messages of a mysterious invented enemy unseen, giant knight or flaming dragon, the intercepter a speck in time facing the immensity of confrontable selves.

And how and where is John? asks Tess.

John has been built by the house of fiction, is admired by sincerity, has elapsed. Perhaps John is Pooh Bear, sitting there dirty gold on the bed, over sixty-five years old, the musical box inside the tum long silent. John is whole languages, eager and easy to please. John is Tess.

A long way from the little girl whispering into the rabbit-hole, slow-uptaker and late-starter in all things, in education, sex, love, writing, driving, divorce, independence; in death maybe, but too late anyway for the latest degenderings. And as flybyable, flowable time has slowly then swiftly extinguished the separate fullnesses of time, only the present fullnesses remain, and the remake of a life becomes more and more impossible.

But then, says Tess with an affectionate hug and a loving laugh at the old lady, a remake is never as good as the original.

172